THEY TOUCHED US
FOR GOOD

Other books by the author

PEARLS OF WISDOM
NUGGETS FOR VICTORIOUS LIVING
STORIES TO WARM YOUR HEART
WISDOM, FAITH AND A SONG

.

This is a book that stirred my heart to the core from the beginning to the end. Kofi has captured here the very important roles that mothers, teachers, and selfless individuals from very humble beginnings have played in the lives of others, especially young people.

One cannot read this book and remain the same.

If I were the head of any school or institution of leadership I would make this book a required textbook. The thoughts and lessons in this book are so captivating you may be tempted to read it at a sitting. I would encourage you to resist that temptation and urge you to read this masterpiece over and over again. You will become wiser and challenged to be an influencing agent for good in our society.

David Hammond,
Former General Secretary, Bible Society of Ghana and
Former Area Secretary for Africa, United Bible Societies

Lessons carefully distilled from the cauldron of life, dispensed with love, guaranteed to impact your life. Highly recommended. If you missed the earlier books by this experienced man who willingly shares from the excursions in his mind and from his earthly peregrinations, then you have another opportunity: grab it with both hands and feet!

Nana Awere Damoah,
Author/Publisher

The author, Kofi Adu Labi, gives a succinct exposé of some pillars of life that are critical for good living and personal development. The writings touch on religion, history, philosophy, business administration, sociology and, above all, biographies. Having read bits and pieces of some writings of the author, I am delighted to see this book as a comprehensive piecing together of some of those thoughts.

Although not a textbook on leadership, *They Touched Us For Good* makes good reading for leadership, and those who yearn for leadership influence cannot afford not to read this book.

Kwabena Boadu Oku-Afari,
Executive Director, African Development Bank

●

Leadership is a very important aspect of human life. This is because every human being has been created by God to rule and have dominion (Gen 1:26) over the earth and everything in it. In essence, we are all created to lead. Leaders are very powerful because their decisions affect them as well as those following or looking up to them.

What actually differentiates powerful leaders from powerless ones is the influence they have. There are some people who occupied leadership roles at a point in their lives but still command so much respect and dignity years after their service. For such persons, even though they no longer occupy their leadership positions, they still have considerable influence over the people they once led. This clearly indicates that leadership is not limited to a term of office, but must endure a lifetime. That said, an enduring influence is not achieved through eloquence, charisma and wealth, but through good character.

The writer has, therefore, done a great job to bring out some exemplary leaders whose genuine character shone bright in their leadership and how they faithfully served in their generation as David did (Acts 13:36). I recommend this book to every individual, particularly the young adults, who want to make an influential impact in their generation. It is never too late to make a difference, and I am confident that this book would be a great resource in this regard.

Alexander Nana Yaw Kumi-Larbi (Apostle),
(General Secretary, The Church of Pentecost)

I have read the book and it is delightful, on many levels. For its idea, content, and style of the author, all of which make delightful reading.

Beyond the book itself, I felt like this was a project which absolutely needed to be done, and finally someone has done it.

It is history, in bite-sized chunks which is easy to read and digest, and crucial for many reasons.

The stories of illustrious people told here are lost on many, especially the younger generation. The author, is an accomplished person in many fields. He is someone I grew up looking up to, and I have always respected his calm, assured leadership and excellence. He has impressed me again with this interesting approach to history. He tells very important true stories in a most relaxed and enjoyable way; a writing style most suited for today's busy person.

This is a very useful project in history and nation-building. It tells the stories of what some of our forebears did to build the Ghana we have today, and to me it suggests what more could be achieved if we followed their footsteps. It is an important approach because if we wait for each story to be written into a history book, we may never get through it. This approach of telling stories of our heroes and heroines in a quick but factual way, bringing out the main points to note about each of them is a really great approach.

The content is fascinating for me, although I knew some of the stories already. They make great reading and excited me all over again. I am sure they will excite and rekindle some fervour in all readers. It reminds us we are a great people and can achieve great things if we put our minds to it.

We need to celebrate our heroes not for their sake but for our own sake. We need to remind ourselves of what has been done in the past with fewer resources so we can remove excuses from our way as we strive to achieve more with the resources and opportunities we have today.

Here is a compendium of stories of great people gone by, which will remind us all that the Black Star of Ghana has always shone bright and we should make it shine brighter. It must be noted that this is not fiction; it is history, it is factual, informative and motivational.

The author does us all a great favour and for that we are truly grateful. Get a copy and get reading. It will edify you for greater works!

Kofi Bentil,
Lawyer, Lecturer, VP ImaniAfrica,
Author

THEY
TOUCHED US
FOR GOOD

Kofi Otutu Adu Labi

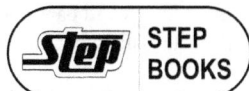

STEP | STEP BOOKS

STEP PUBLISHERS
Accra, Ghana

THEY TOUCHED US FOR GOOD
Copyright © 2017, Kofi Otutu Adu Labi

ISBN 978-9988-8629-0-9

Published by
STEP PUBLISHERS
P. O. Box AN 11150, Accra-North, Ghana
stepwriters@gmail.com. www.stepbooks.org
Tel. +233 (0)302 513487

Cover design and page layout by
Sam Nyarko-Mensah (samadonia@yahoo.com)

8

CONTENTS

to

all the leaders who have influenced me for good, with special reference to Mr S. T. Ampofo, who is listed among the greats highlighted in this book.

ACKNOWLEDGEMENTS

I acknowledge the debt of gratitude I owe to all those who read my first three books. The reactions to the books, *Stories to Warm Your Heart, Pearls of Wisdom* and *Nuggets for Victorious Living,* have been most humbling and very encouraging. I have sometimes found them overwhelming. They keep coming even as I am completing the manuscript for this title, the fifth book I am releasing.

The words of encouragement and the testimonies from many about how lessons from the books have been a blessing and source of empowerment to them, have in no small measure been the inspiration for this and the fourth book titled *Wisdom, Faith and a Song.*

My prayer is that this, and my four other books, will be a source of inspiration to all who read them, and that their lives will be enriched greatly.

FOREWORD

As an ardent reader of books on transformational leadership, I find this book by the author a useful resource that should complement existing works on leadership. The title itself, *They Touched Us For Good* stimulates reading interest right from the start, and not to mention the writing style. I have enjoyed all the three books by the author—*Stories to Warm Your Heart*, *Pearls of Wisdom* and *Nuggets for Victorious Living*. These have been a source of encouragement and inspiration to me personally, and I will recommend all three to anyone.

In this new work, the author delves deep into history and uses personal encounters with people and events to draw up important lessons. These are used to derive very critical but less-mentioned elements for defining what, how and why leadership matters in every aspect of our lives; in the family, at work, in a fellowship and even at personal level. For me, the phrase in the book "I have come to believe that life is about leaving an impact . . . It is about making a difference for the good in people," summarises it all.

As a matter of fact, I am not surprised by the author's ability to simplify complexities of life into practical lessons that readers can easily relate to. I have personally known the author as an experienced public servant with over thirty-five years of work experience in banking; a passionate reader of history and literature, and a mentor to many—including my good self.

The statement in the book, "Work is central to our lives . . . we work for our self-esteem," aptly ushers readers into the mind of the author and demonstrates the professional leanings by the author who I have known during his work at the Bank of Ghana. I can therefore affirm that his principal assertion that "Leadership should be about influence," is a statement he has lived to the benefit of many, including myself.

Certainly, readers of books on leadership would surely find this book intriguing because of the practicality and the easy style. The author's careful combination of history, literature, international diplomacy, and humour makes reading very enjoyable. Also, by using elements of suspense and poetry, the book has the savour of a novel which gives it a unique identity in the league of books on leadership.

It is my great pleasure to commend this book as a must-read.

Dr Johnson P. Asiama,
Second Deputy Governor, Bank of Ghana
July 24, 2017

INTRODUCTION

I have come to believe that life is about leaving an impact, a positive impact at that, on people. It is about making a difference for the good in people. Life should be about spending time and relating with others in such a way that they go away better as a result of their paths having crossed with yours.

Leadership should be about influence. Anyone can exercise authority as a result of the position they occupy or are appointed to. People may feel obliged to take their instructions for the simple reason that doing otherwise may lead to unpleasant consequences. Such leaders do not leave lasting influences that are favourable and beneficial.

Leadership should be about influence. Influence that is positively impactful, lasting and cross-generational.

This has clear implications to those who see leadership from the perspective of influence, and not position, power or authority. This involves a style of leading and managing people with an eternal viewpoint. It sees leadership as a unique opportunity to mould lives. It sees leadership as a role-modelling function. It sees leadership as a trans-generational responsibility to touch lives for good and to help develop responsible men and women of the future.

The type of leadership we are discussing does not seek its own interests. Rather the primary concern is the nurturing of the potential the leader sees in the lives of the people he is responsible for. The nurturing can take various forms. It can be channelled through formal settings and also informal ones. In other cases, this can be advanced through conversations and personal relationships.

This book looks at the lives of some of the people I count among the greatest leaders of our times, and times past. They may not be listed among those who are the subject of case studies in business schools. But they are among the great and real leaders whose styles we should emulate because they touched lives, and are still touching lives, in ways that are boundless, permanent and beneficial.

The world needs more of such leaders. You can become like them as you read this book and make a decision to put into practice the examples they left behind.

Thank you for deciding to come along with me on this journey.

1
WATCH THESE THINGS

D o not rush through life. Take your time to observe and reflect on the everyday activities around you. You will learn a lot about the meaning of life and what role you can play in it.

"If you live in the world and you do not do something to benefit others, you are a parasite." These are the words of Professor James Ephraim, former Vice Chancellor of the Catholic University of Ghana, Fiapre.

He made this profound statement at a "Republic Day" choral concert organised by the WitsHarmonic Choir Ghana at the Christ the King Hall in Accra in July 2016. My wife Elioenai and I were privileged to be among the guests who included Emeritus Prof. J. H. Kwabena Nketia. The choir, under the direction of its founder, Witsfield Kwablah, treated the gathering to a number of compositions by the founder based on patriotic, philosophical and folkloric themes. Prof. Ephraim advised that the youth should keep asking themselves, "What can I do for someone else to benefit from?" In that connection, Prof. Ephraim advised that the young people of today should seek to do the following to be useful to society:

- they must carry a heart of excellence;
- they must learn to respect, tolerate and accommodate different views;
- they must learn to listen with the ears of their hearts; and
- they must aim at living for the common good.

An evening very well spent, I must say.

MEET AWELENGA LABILA, 104 YEARS OLD!

On Ghana's Independence Day holiday in March 2016, I visited an elderly man who lives in my neighbourhood. This is an elderly man my friend Ambassador James Naadjie and I see relaxing in front of his home during our regular morning walks every now and then. We have been exchanging pleasantries with him, but that day was the first time that I sat down to have a chat with him.

I am referring to Mr Awelenga Labila, who said that he was 104 (yes, 104) years old and going on to 105! I asked for evidence to back up his age claim. He did not have documentary evidence but went on to take me through his background, an exercise which turned out to be fascinating.

This is what Awelenga Labila had to say: He was born at Bawku, in the Upper East Region of Ghana early in the 20th century. He grew up at Bawku, but did not have formal education. At the outbreak of the Second World War (1939), which he referred to as "the General de Gaulle war", he moved south to Kumasi to work as a labourer. After a short stay in Kumasi, he travelled further south to Aboso in the Western Region to work as an underground miner. He also worked with a surveyor undertaking surveys for mineral deposits.

HOW HE FIRST HEARD OF THE STRUGGLE
FOR POLITICAL INDEPENDENCE AND
KWAME NKRUMAH

My centenarian friend, Awelenga Labila, said that from Aboso he went to Prestea (in the same part of the country as Aboso) where he resumed work as a miner. By the way, that part of Ghana is richly endowed with precious minerals, including gold, diamonds and manganese. There are still substantial mining operations there by both big-time corporates and small-scale miners, some operating illegally in what is known in the local parlance as 'galamsey' mining.

While he was in Prestea, he started hearing of agitations for political independence for the Gold Coast, as Ghana was then known. There was one man in particular whose name he kept hearing. That name was Kwame Nkrumah. There were other names, he said, and these included J. B. Danquah, Paa Grant and Akufo-Addo.

What he heard was that Kwame Nkrumah was the youngest among the people leading the push for freedom from colonial rule. He had arrived in the country after completing his studies in the United States.

According to him, Kwame Nkrumah was hosted by Komla Gbedemah when the former first arrived in the Gold Coast.

As an aside, let me say that I met and dealt with Komla Gbedemah in a professional capacity in the 1980s. This was a name that was very well known from pre- and post-independence days. I had never expected to meet him face to face, but as fate would have it, I handled a matter for him, and what a wonderful experience that was for me! I found him to be a perfect gentleman. He was also a stickler for punctuality and paid attention to details. Yes, details! How we need people who pay attention to details! He had a ramrod straight appearance in his neatly tailored suits. Dealing with him was a learning and pleasant experience.

Now back to the narration on my centenarian

Did Awelenga Labila ever see Nkrumah at close quarters beyond hearing his name as one of those at the forefront of the call for independence, I asked?

To answer the question he took me back to a meeting he says he attended at the residence of the local Kusasi chief at Prestea in the late 1940s. He, Awelenga Labila, is a Kusasi from Bawku and so he felt obliged to attend that meeting. At that meeting, one Mr Asumda (a Kusasi teacher based at Bawku at the time), who later became a high ranking official in Nkrumah's government after independence in 1957, gave the gathering a briefing on the struggle for independence. He then asked them to throw their support behind Nkrumah.

Awelenga responded to the call cheerfully and became a foot soldier of Nkrumah, he told me. From Prestea he moved to the port city of Takoradi, this time to work as a cook while at the same time espousing the cause of Nkrumah and independence. As a result of these activities, he had the opportunity to meet Nkrumah on a number of occasions.

He described Kwame Nkrumah as a man of the people, who mixed freely with them. He claims that he was slightly older than Nkrumah, who he described as his master.

Mr Awelenga Labila appeared to be a keen observer of Ghana's history and had some views on contemporary Ghana.

AWELENGA LABILA ON CONTEMPORARY GHANA

My centenarian friend had very strong views on what he said he had seen and heard, and kept seeing and hearing, about Ghana.

First of all, he bemoaned what he saw as a lack of love and devotion by Ghanaians to their country. 'We do not love Ghana!' he exclaimed. He would like to see the type of passion that he and others had in their time at work in the current generation of citizens. That passion led them to make sacrifices for the country without always thinking of their personal interests first. He advised that we should take our destiny into our own hands, as the consequences could be dire if we failed to do so.

Already he was seeing and hearing of many areas of the economy being taken over by foreigners. He was not a happy person, and he knew Kwame Nkrumah would not have allowed this to happen. He was of the view that this should not be allowed to continue. We should dictate how things should be done, he continued. He made specific reference to the devastation being caused to our water bodies by the activities of illegal (galamsey) miners, some of who are reported to have foreign partners.

Mr Awelenga Labila called for agriculture to be taken more seriously and given more support so that we can produce all the food we need and not have to import any. He had fond memories of the 'Operation Feed Yourself' days of the General Acheampong era in the mid-1970s. Those were the days when we attained food sufficiency with our staples like maize, rice and yam, to mention only the obvious ones. It was his wish that more attention and resources would be devoted to creating jobs for the young people of Ghana. He said that this was the vision of his mentor Kwame Nkrumah and this is what guided his blueprint for the industrialisation of Ghana.

What was the secret behind his longevity? His answer was simple but significant. There is nothing like a wholesome and balanced diet, he said. He was careful as to what he ate. He had always believed in standing up for the truth, and he abhorred gossip and backstabbing. Above all, he ascribed everything to the grace of God. Yes, he is a Christian, he said, and looks forward to going to heaven. He has two living children and many grandchildren and great-grandchildren.

LISTEN TO DR FELIX KONOTEY-AHULU

I have always insisted that Dr Felix Konotey-Ahulu, Prof. F. K. A. Allotey and former United Nations Secretary General, Nobel Laureate Kofi Annan are the greatest living Ghanaians. If anyone has another list, I shall be pleased to take a look at it.

I take everything Dr Konotey-Ahulu writes seriously and I want to share one at this juncture. He always writes in such a way that his messages stick with you. This time he was writing about Cameron Duodu in a post he shared on achimota2010@googlegroups.com.

Cameron Duodu is one of the greatest writers this country has produced. He has an eye for details and a wicked sense of humour. He is aged now, and lives in London, but contributes columns to the *Ghanaian Times* and the *Daily Guide*, among others, regularly.

When I was a law student at the University of Ghana in the early 1970s I had the privilege of serving on a three-member studio panel of the then external service of the Ghana Broadcasting Corporation (GBC). The discussions were followed by listeners in many parts of Africa. It was a joy and a learning experience to listen to the erudition of Cameron Duodu who was on that panel. The third member was Ray Kakraba-Quashie.

Now back to the post by Dr Felix Konotey-Ahulu

"I pray that God Almighty give the likes of Cameron Duodu long life, with all his cerebral faculties intact so that he can remind and educate those half his age who are directing our national affairs, and the rest of us about 59 years ago and earlier.

You see, while I was out of the Gold Coast on the day our country became Ghana, Cameron was standing a few feet away from the Founder of the Nation, Mr Kwame Nkrumah, later Osagyefo Dr Kwame Nkrumah.

(Incidentally on that day, March 6, 1957 in the afternoon I was playing 'Inside Left' for Westminster School of Medicine

First Eleven against another London University Medical School and I scored 3 goals in quick succession earning me the nickname 'Black Flash', the name then reserved for Roy Ankrah, Featherweight Champion.)

But back to Cameron. The man does his homework, and we must learn to thank God for him. We must go further: we must go digging into our archives—at least the *Daily Graphic* and *Ghanaian Times* archives and bring out things Ghanaians have done of enormous significance. These things were published. If the *British Medical Journal* has electronically produced material published since the year 1840 AD why cannot our national papers do the same, so that kith and kin in California, Tasmania, and Johannesburg can learn about significant events published decades ago?

Just one example: Do Ghanaians know that but for Dr Reginald Addae (Castle Road Clinic) and Dr Frank Djabanor (St Luke's Clinic), all black people could be stopped at international airports and be tested for sickle cells before flying?

This ('Tafracher') nonsense of a recommendation published in a leading international medical journal was endorsed in *London Times* and in the scientific journal NATURE. It took these 2 London University-trained Ghanaian physicians to expose a scientific fraud and get the publication for the recommendation withdrawn forthwith!

Why, Dr Djabanor asked, did the medical journal single out 'all Negro travellers' for this most unscientific recommendation when it was known that white people in an area of Greece had more sickle cells than anywhere in Ghana? Dr Reg Addae's research found that the article was based on a fraud, and both he and Frank Djabanor wrote to the medical journal proving evidence of fraud. Their influence was felt across the Atlantic at Kennedy Airport where black pilots and aircrew who had been grounded because they had Sickle Cell Trait were promptly reinstated.

Now, this huge Ghanaian achievement was published in a blow by blow account in the *Ghanaian Times* whose Editor was the late Mr Gyawu-Kyem. Wanted today are Ghanaians half the age of Cameron Duodu who in my opinion deserves a Doctorate—yes, wanted today are young Ghanaians with an equally keen eye for historical detail—to educate and teach us from the archives.

(By the way, I wrote to Mr E. R. Dwemoh, the then Boss of Kotoka International Airport and our Civil Aviation to recommend to the Board that Drs Addae and Djabanor be given free First Class travel on Ghana Airways. I am not sure of the outcome.)

I do hope, come 2017 God willing, we shall be told that all past copies of our major newspapers are online so we can judge our plus and minus achievements since independence. Health policy-wise though, I can say categorically that no foreign scientists had the nerve to come to us in those days to dictate what research needed doing and what not. Some of us at Korle-Bu even told the W.H.O. what WE wanted done, and we did not tamely acquiesce to what THEY wanted done.

Pray for Cameron and those on his wavelength."

Very insightful and enlightening, I must say.

ALISTAIR COOKE AND LETTER FROM AMERICA

I have always loved radio. I suspect that many of my generation have the same love. I am referring to listening to wholesome broadcasts, educational, informative and truly entertaining in value.

I got a radio all to myself at university, and I could therefore listen to my favourite programmes. Apart from the local Ghana Broadcasting Corporation (GBC), which was all there was, I listened to Radio Elwa (based in Liberia) for religious broadcasts from Billy Graham, the VOA and above all, the BBC.

The BBC was the gold standard for news and pure enlightenment. I dare say it still is. I loved listening to the annual promenade concerts (the Proms) and the *Brain of Britain*, a nationwide general knowledge contest, in addition to programmes hosted by presenters like Roy Plomley and Jonathan Dimbleby.

But by far the programme that I looked forward to on the BBC was the weekly *Letter from America* by Alistair Cooke. I listened to this programme for probably thirty years. *Letter from America* was a weekly 15-minute radio series broadcast on BBC Radio 4 and to the world through the BBC World Service. Throughout its history, it was presented by Alistair Cooke, who would speak of a topical issue in the USA, tying together different strands of observation and anecdote and often ending on a humorous or poignant note. The series ran from 24 March 1946 to 20 February 2004, making it the longest-running speech radio programme in history. I must say that I loved listening to Alistair Cooke and to his sharp observations and cryptic analysis of news and events in the United States and the world at large.

How I wished we had someone like that to give a weekly *Letter from Ghana*, on radio, to the outside world! Seniors K. B. Asante and Cameron Duodu, I hope you are listening.

ALISTAIR COOKE AND 'LETTER FROM AMERICA'
Tell him he is not President!

My weekends were never complete without tuning in to listen to *Letter from America* by Alistair Cooke. If he were alive today, he would have been providing us with week by week commentary on Donald Trump, Vladimir Putin, Kim Jong-un, Hillary Clinton and others and on the real issues and influences behind the news making the world stage.

On 2 March 2004, at the age of 95, following advice from his doctors, Cooke announced his retirement from *Letter from America*. That was the end of an era. He died less than a month later, on 30 March 2004, at his home in New York City. He was born British, but became a naturalised American after he moved to the United States.

One particular *Letter from America* that is still etched in my mind related to a famous election night in 1916 when, by the time the eastern states were reporting their votes, it became very clear that the Republican candidate, Charles Evans Hughes, had won handsomely over the Democrat, Woodrow Wilson. His supporters had started celebrating. Though most other results were in, California had yet to be heard from. At about two in the morning, however, all the results were in. By then an exultant Hughes had retired to bed, firm in the assurance that he had bagged the United States Presidency.

A Washington reporter telephoned Mr Hughes, wanting to speak to him urgently. Instead of Hughes, the reporter heard an irritated voice at the other end. It was Mr Hughes' butler who said, 'The President has gone to bed and cannot be disturbed.' I shall never forget how Alistair Cooke concluded that broadcast. The reporter on the line, he said in that unique, deep and sonorous voice of his, told the butler, 'Better wake him up and tell him he's not President!'

The enduring lesson for me? Beware of presumption! Do not be quick to jump to conclusions.

WAKE HIM UP. HE HAS NO RIGHT TO BE SLEEPING!

A true story, this time from Ghana, but it is not about elections. The year was 1983. Economic conditions were not good and a terrible drought had worsened matters. The then government entered into a Ghana/Brazil technical co-operation for trade relations between the two countries.

As part of the arrangement, agreement was reached for the supply of agricultural goods and machinery, vehicles and assorted items on concessionary terms to Ghana from Brazil. My employers at the time, the Social Security Bank (later SSB Bank and now Societé Generale Ghana) were the implementing bank. After all arrangements had been concluded for the shipment of the equipment and other items, we received a cable from Rio de Janeiro that the ship carrying the goods had developed some problems and had been forced to anchor off the north-eastern coast of Brazil. This was a shocking piece of news to us, as a lot of expectations had been raised in the country about the likely impact the items were going to have on agriculture in particular. That is how come Mr John Bentum-Williams, Managing Director of SSB Bank at the time, called me to his office and asked me to accompany him to see the Brazilian Ambassador to Ghana. The purpose of the visit was to ask him to do everything possible to get the items transhipped under a certificate of emergency. We did not find him at the office. The time was about 3 pm. We therefore proceeded to his residence where we were told by his housekeeper that he was taking a rest.

Mr John Bentum-Williams (much later High Commissioner to Malaysia and India) then exclaimed, 'Go and wake him up. He has no right to be sleeping.' I cannot remember whether I giggled or kept a straight-face. The poor housekeeper went and woke up the Ambassador from his nap and we agreed a line of action to resolve the problem that had arisen. I was despatched to Brazil the very next day, along with an official from the Bank of Ghana, and to cut a long story short (and indeed it is a long story), matters were resolved and the goods arrived in Ghana to everyone's delight.

Those who sleep, sleep at night. Indeed, there are times when you have no right to be sleeping!

> "The quality of a person's life is in direct proportion to their commitment to excellence, regardless of their chosen field of endeavour." — Vince Lombardi

> "Whatever you do, work heartily, as for the Lord and not for men" (Col 3:23 ESV).

The application? Be faithful, diligent and give your all to that little, seemingly insignificant and unglamorous job. You will get fulfilment, sleep well at night and beyond that, your recognition and reward will surely follow when you least expect it.

"True happiness . . . is not attained through self-gratification, but through fidelity to a worthy purpose." —Helen Keller

"Success in life is a matter not so much of talent or opportunity as of concentration and perseverance." — C. W. Wendte

Bear this in mind as you go about your affairs.

"The simple virtues of willingness, readiness, alertness, and courtesy will carry a young man farther than mere smartness." — Henry Davison

I can testify, from my experience, that this is true. It pays to be courteous, willing to be of assistance, ready and alert to meet the needs of your customers.

In my days as a young professional, I derived a lot of energy and motivation from letters (yes, letters, and some coming from outside Ghana) from people thanking me for what they said had been a considerate and helpful way in addressing their needs. I must confess that in some cases I did not even recollect what exactly I had done. Am I blowing my own trumpet, to use local English? I hope not. I am only sharing from my experience to let you know that it pays to be courteous, alert, ready and willing to help those you meet in the course of duty. Even if you are not able to solve their problems, they will leave your presence with a good experience.

"TIME AND TIDE WAIT FOR NO MAN" —GEOFFREY CHAUCER

I still remember Chaucer's *Canterbury Tales* from my secondary school English Literature courses. Characters in the tales portrayed different virtues and characteristics. Things that we can learn from and others that we should avoid.

Time and tide waiting for no one is one enduring lesson. The picture is very graphic. Whoever saw time or tide waiting because someone decided that he or she was not ready? Such a person will surely miss the boat.

The reality is that you will never 'find' time for anything. Instead you must 'make' time for the things that are important to you.

> "More often than not it is in the quiet, unnoticed, unapplauded realms of life that one demonstrates integrity—within the walls of one's own home—in the secret chambers of one's own heart." — Charles Swindoll, in his book *Rise and Shine.*

This is what character is about. Let us be genuine with ourselves and especially at home, when all the defences are down, and we shall influence the next generation far more than we could imagine.

> "People with integrity walk safely, but those who follow crooked paths will be exposed" (Prov 10:9 NLT).

"Consistency: It's the jewel worth wearing; It's the anchor worth weighing; It's the thread worth weaving; It's a battle worth winning." — Charles R. Swindoll

A good name is worth more than gold. So is a reputation for consistency. Let your consistency show in your trustworthiness, reliability, resilience and stability. When it gets to the crunch, your consistency will be your reward.

"And let us not grow weary while doing good, for in due season we shall reap if we do not lose heart" (Gal 6:9 NKJV).

"If one should desire to know whether a kingdom is well-governed, if its morals are good or bad, the quality of its music will furnish the answer . . . Character is the backbone of our human culture, and music is the flowering of character." — Confucius (551-479 BC), Chinese social philosopher

"By education, I do not mean simply learning. I mean the training in mind, in morals, and in hand that helps to make one socially efficient. Not simply the three R's, but the three H's: the head, the hand, and the heart." — Aggrey of Africa

Education should train for character and relevance. It should make the recipient whole. Let us listen to our revered

Aggrey who made this profound statement almost 100 years ago.

WHEN LEICESTER CITY BECAME BARCLAYS PREMIER LEAGUE CHAMPIONS IN 2016

What lessons?

Against all odds, Leicester City Football Club won the English premier league in 2016. This was the first time in its 132-year history. I suspect that if anyone had predicted what happened at the beginning of the season, that person would have been laughed to scorn. The team has never been one of the greats in English football and were relegation-bound the previous year. I took an interest in them because there were at least two Ghanaians in their first team. According to a BBC report, they were a team of cast-offs and bargain buys written off before the season had started, led by a manager who had been sacked in five of his previous jobs. And yet see how far they had come. They did what Napoleon could not do!

What lessons are there for us? As individuals? As corporate entities? As a nation? First, we should not allow anyone to look down on us, whatever our background or circumstances may be. Second, we should believe in ourselves. Third, we should refuse to be intimidated by the 'Giants' of this world. They are also flesh and blood like us, and whatever they have achieved in the past we can also achieve. Fourth, no one is beyond redemption. Even if you are down, you can be restored if you do not give up. Finally, remember the words of the Preacher:

"Better is the end of a thing than the beginning of it, and the patient in spirit is better than the proud in spirit" (Eccl 7:8 AMP).

ARE WE SEEING THE BEST THAT WE CAN BE?

"It is not the style of clothes one wears, neither the kind of automobile one drives, nor the amount of money one has in the bank that counts. These mean nothing. It is simply service that measures success." — George Washington Carver

George Washington Carver was a prominent African American scientist and inventor. Carver developed hundreds of products using the peanut (groundnut), sweet potatoes and soybeans. He died in 1943. He believed in agricultural education. Though he was born into slavery, he left a legacy of ingenuity and the transformative power of education. We were not born into slavery (thankfully) and have not had to face the type of odds Carver faced. Let us therefore get really serious and determine to be of service to the present age and to posterity.

What, for example, are we doing to utilise the potentials of the numerous plants, vegetables, fruits and crops that grow so abundantly year round in Ghana? Are we seeing the best that we can do? Or are we just interested in the short-term benefits that may accrue to us through wanton exploitation of non-renewable natural resources, which come with heavy collateral damage?

"And He said to them, 'Take heed and beware of covetousness, for one's life does not consist in the abundance of the things he possesses'" (Lk 12:15 NKJV).

EXCUSES!

"Ninety-nine per cent of the failures come from people who have the habit of making excuses."
— George Washington Carver

Indeed, excuses may sound good and ease that guilty feeling of not (never?) getting started, but you will end nowhere with them.

Stop the excuses. Do something, and do it today.

2

SHARPENING
YOUR SAW

Your story is being written as the moments pass away. Make sure you leave a mark. Do not just pass through the world. There is something that you can do to make this a better place.

SAYING GOODBYE TO A DISTINGUISHED GHANAIAN, PAATII OFOSU-AMAAH

In May 2016, my wife Elioenai and I joined hundreds of mourners to bid farewell to Mr Paatii Ofosu-Amaah, a truly distinguished Ghanaian who had had an outstanding career at the World Bank. At the World Bank, where he worked for 30 years, he established himself as an internationally respected legal expert. He rose to the top echelons there, becoming a Vice President, Deputy General Counsel and Corporate Secretary. He was a counsellor to three World Bank Presidents including James Wolfensohn and Robert Zoellick. On retiring from the World Bank in 2007, he was headhunted to become Special Adviser to the President of the African Development Bank till 2015. From there he was invited to be a member of the African Union High Level Panel negotiating between Sudan and South Sudan. He was also on the boards of the African University of Science and Technology and the Nelson Mandela Institution, among other roles he played.

Paatii was two years ahead of me at university. I found him and his lovely wife, Waafas, to be most gracious people. I had the delight of being received by them in their Maryland home during visits to Washington DC in my earlier working life. They complemented each other well with their respect for other people, while maintaining principled stands. The funeral service at the Accra Ridge Church saw many dignitaries from different parts of the world in attendance. Former President John Kufuor of Ghana was present, as was a high level delegation from the African Union led by former President Abubakar of Nigeria. Paatii was the last-born in a family of achievers. It was painful to see his distinguished elder siblings, including Prof. G. K. A. Ofosu-Amaah (our former Dean at Law School) bidding farewell to their youngest brother. He served his generation well. He has left a legacy worth emulating.

> "Better to spend your time at funerals than at parties. After all, everyone dies—so the living should take this to heart" (Eccl 7:2 NLT).

A CHANCE MEETING WITH REV. PROFESSOR GILBERT ANSRE

I ran into Reverend Professor Gilbert Ansre unexpectedly as I was leaving a shopping centre in Accra one day. This is someone I have known from a distance since entering the University of Ghana as a freshman resident of Akuafo Hall in October 1970. He became Hall Master after the late Prof. Ayikwei Bulley had completed his term.

He was a fixture and a reassuring presence at all the Sunday evening services at the Akuafo Hall chapel at which I was a regular participant.

Prof. Ansre is well known and respected in higher educational and theological circles. Over the past three or more decades however, he has become even better known as a world-renowned Bible translator and scholar. He remains a Consultant to the United Bible Societies.

It was good meeting him and to speak with him, but the best was yet to come! Imagine my delight when he told me that he used to spend his holidays at Abiriw, my hometown, in the 1930s! He mentioned the name of the family he used to spend time with then, and needless to say, this is a family I am closely connected to. I did not have the courage to ask for his age, but if he was spending holidays on the Akuapem ridge in the 1930s as a school boy (and knowing the people he mentioned), he must be about 90 years old. He looks as fit as a fiddle! Thanks be to God. Pleasant memories, I keep saying, are the joys of life.

"Those who are planted in the house of the LORD
Shall flourish in the courts of our God. They shall

still bear fruit in old age; They shall be fresh and flourishing" (Ps 92:13-14 NKJV).

AN EVENING WITH NOBEL LAUREATE KOFI ANNAN

The auditorium of the College of Physicians and Surgeons in Accra, Ghana, was bursting at the seams one July evening in 2016. The reason? Ghana's only Nobel Peace Laureate, was giving a lecture on "Credible and Peaceful Elections: A Prerequisite for Africa's Progress."

Kofi Annan served as Secretary General of the United Nations from 1997 to 2006. He is without doubt the most famous living Ghanaian.

Let me share a few of the gems I picked up from his address, held under the auspices of the *Kronti ne Akwamu* Lecture series. They are not exact quotes but still capture the essence of what he said.

Democracy is too important to be left to politicians alone. We must not let the street take the place of the ballot box. We need credible elections, elections with integrity. Democracy is never fully achieved. We need to deepen democracy on an ongoing basis.

At the end of the day it does not matter which party or candidate wins, as long as the country wins.

It was an evening very well spent. My sister, Judge Akua Kuenyehia, formerly of the International Criminal Court, The Hague, was the Chairperson for the occasion. I had the privilege of meeting our Kofi Annan in the company of my sister afterwards and I gave him autographed copies of my three books which had been launched a few days before our encounter.

Kofi Annan does have a fine sense of humour. When it was time for him to be introduced before he mounted the rostrum, the Master of Ceremonies stated that this was not someone who needed an introduction and that he doubted if there was anyone in the auditorium who did not know who Kofi Annan was.

That was certainly a statement of fact. However, Mr Kofi Annan had something to say in response. He narrated how after retiring from serving as UN Secretary General for 10 years, he decided to take a good, long rest. He and Mrs Nane Annan (his Swedish-born wife) therefore retreated to an isolated cottage at the edge of a thick forest in Italy. They had no TV, no radio, no telephone and no newspapers. Can you imagine this? They were going to spend six weeks at this edenic location. He was now a free man! Freedom! How sweet it must have sounded.

After a week however, they had had enough of this Stone Age existence (my own coinage) and he decided that they should make a foray into a small shop in a nearby village to get newspapers, after all. He could not take the complete isolation any more. I could identify with that, as I cannot imagine how I can survive without my daily diet of newspapers. As soon as they entered the small shop, they felt all eyes on them and the few people there started whispering to each other. In a moment one of them walked up to him and exclaimed, "Hey, Morgan Freeman, I need your autograph." On completing their mission at the shop, his wife Nane told him: 'You are now truly free.'

By the way, Morgan Freeman is a well-known American actor and narrator. I googled him after the lecture and did not fail to notice his striking resemblance to Kofi Annan. What an evening!

BREAKING THE MYTH

My Grandfather's clock was too large for the shelf,
So it stood ninety years on the floor;
It was taller by half than the old man himself,
Though it weighed not a penny-weight more.
It was bought on the morn of the day that he was born.
And was always his treasure and pride.
But it stopped short, never to go again
When the old man died.
Ninety years without slumbering,
Tick, tock, tick, tock,
His life seconds numbering,
Tick, tock, tick, tock,
It stopped short, never to go again
When the old man died.

Talk about memories again. Watch your memories. They are life enriching or life negating. They are history too. The Winneba Youth Choir were singing this old song and I felt renewed joy flooding my body and relieving me of the fatigue I was feeling one particular evening.

At Ofori Panin, Mr S. T. Ampofo (Headmaster) actually held a big clock with him and used the pendulum any time we got to the tick, tock section of this song. The occasion was an evening of musical performances dubbed "Breaking the Myth" at the auditorium of the College of Physicians and Surgeons in Accra.

The groups, of young musicians, were the Winneba Youth Choir, BASICS International (Brothers and Sisters in Christ Serving), Achievers Ghana Education and the Pan African Youth Orchestra.

There was drama, dance, piano and violin with Bible verses, flute performances and music for the gong gong. Remember Ephraim (Owura) Amu?

The event attracted lots of people and was also used to raise funds to help young people in disadvantaged communities to break the myth of illiteracy and poverty and let them see how, through the love of God exhibited by concerned members of society, they can rise above their limitations. It was a joy to see the musicians, some as young as six years old, displaying dexterity on various musical instruments.

We expressed our thanks to the chief sponsor for the event, Mrs Matilda Amissah-Arthur (the Guest of Honour at my Trilogy Launch) for her passion to see disadvantaged young people helped out of poverty through the tools of reading and music, accompanied by the Word of God.

> "You have taught children and infants to tell of your strength, silencing your enemies and all who oppose you" (Ps 8:2 NLT).

LESSONS FROM THE VICTORY BUSINESS SUMMIT AND FAIR 2016

> "There is no adversity capable of stopping you once the choice to persevere is made." — Jason Kilar

"The perceived negative events of our past should be a platform to launch the success of our future."

That was Dr Ama Boohene-Andah, speaking at the 2016 edition of the Victory Business Summit and Fair held every Republic Day (July 1) at the Victory Congregation of the Presbyterian Church of Ghana, Fafraha. Other speakers at the event were Dr Pearl Aba Scott of the Korle-Bu Teaching Hospital, Mr Paul Anomah-Kodieh (a visually impaired television talk show and news presenter) and Mr Joseph Siaw Agyepong, founder of the Jospong and Zoomlion Groups with companies based in Ghana and other countries. A most inspiring experience, rounded off with a business fair at which church members exhibited products and services from their own (and in most cases small) businesses.

Mr Joseph Siaw Agyepong (Mr Jospong) gave a presentation entitled "Diversification in Business: Lessons from my Life." He held participants spellbound with his story which he dubbed "From trash to cash." We learnt from him that we must do all we can to be among the "Early Morning people" who are always eager to work and thus get rewarded with opportunities. We should not be standing idle, waiting for opportunities to come to us.

Dr Ama Boohene-Andah gave a scintillating testimony about her life. She told us that there is no adversity stopping you once the choice to persevere is made.

We should avoid tunnel vision and dare to dream. Do whatever you find yourself doing well. This may lead you to places you never imagined. No wonder she became the President's (President J. A. Kufuor) physician at a young age.

Mr Paul Anomah-Kordieh, a visually impaired TV newscaster and show presenter, took participants through

43

"Using Communication to develop your Business." We learnt from him that the success and sustenance of our business depends on its effective communication with our internal and external publics.

From Dr Pearl Aba Scott-Jackson, we learnt much about some of the most feared cancers which afflict both men and women. Participants were educated on the various symptoms that will alert them to the early signs to watch out for in staying cancer-free. A healthy body, after all, adds value to a healthy business.

STAND UP FOR SOMETHING

> "It takes nothing to join the crowd; it takes everything to stand alone." — Hans F. Hansen

It is Winston Churchill who said, "You have enemies? Good. It means you've stood up for something, sometime in your life."

Stand up for the right. Be a person of integrity. Refuse to join the bandwagon of stealing the time and resources of the state and your employer. Do not bend the rules to your advantage. If you desire to get involved in partisan politics, to cite only one example, do so because you want to serve and make a difference in the lives of your people and not because it is the opportunity for you also to enrich yourself through patronage.

You may stand vilified in a corrupt society where dishonesty is a way of life, but you would have made a difference, if you prove yourself to be uncompromising in your integrity. Have the guts to stand up for a good cause. Stand up for godly principles. If enough numbers stand up for what is right, our society will change for the better and structures and institutions will work as they should. And the blame game will stop.

> "Do not follow the crowd in doing wrong" (Ex 23:2a NIV).

Be bold

> "There is a stubbornness about me that never can bear to be frightened at the will of others. My courage always rises at every attempt to intimidate me." — Jane Austen, *Pride and Prejudice*

We need more of such an attitude. Be bold. Be principled. Be consistent in your value systems. Refuse to be intimidated and coerced into doing what you know is wrong.

REV. PETER BARKER

Edited version of biography of Rev. Peter Barker, who died in May 2016, London, written by Ross Campbell of the Ghana Evangelism Committee. A service of thanksgiving was held in his honour at the Kaneshie Congregation of the Presbyterian Church of Ghana.

Never heard of him? Read on

Rev. Peter Barker was born in Feltham, UK. In 1939 at age 11, Peter was accepted as a Winchester cathedral choir boy where he spent the next three years. After further schooling at St Edwards in Oxford, between October 1946 and May 1949 Peter did two and a half years' national service in the army and was posted to East Africa. In East Africa, Peter began the practice of reading the Bible, a chapter a day, and listen to sermons broadcast from Nairobi Cathedral—one of which led him in 1948 to give his life to Christ.

On returning to the UK, Peter read History at Oxford (1949-53), and then trained as a journalist (1953-55) with a view to fulfilling the call he felt to return to Africa to work for the Lord. In 1955 Peter came to Ghana for the first time to edit a monthly Christian youth magazine for secondary schools called *New Nation* which he did from 1955 to 1957.

From 1957 to 1960, Peter taught at Okuapemman School, Akropong Akuapem and joined the Christ Church Presbyterian Congregation at Akropong before moving to Labone Secondary School where he taught English, French and history until he felt that God was calling him to full-time preaching of the gospel.

In February 1960, jointly with Nigel Sylvester of Scripture Union, Peter coordinated a visit by Dr Billy Graham for crusade meetings in Ghana.

Also in 1960 Peter offered himself to the Presbyterian Church of Ghana and, following a year of part-time study in London, Peter returned to Ghana and studied for his Bachelor of Divinity (BD) at the Trinity Theological College.

In July 1963 Peter was ordained as a Presbyterian Church of Ghana minister—the first expatriate to do so in the PCG. Peter went on to spend 22 years in the PCG ministry including 18 years involved in founding and managing Asempa Publishers.

In August 1963 Peter and Laura, who had met some years earlier, at St Stephen's church in Twickenham (UK), were married.

Returning to Ghana together in 1963, Peter and Laura served in the Kaneshie Presbyterian Church until 1966.

From 1963 to 1966 while serving the Kaneshie Church, Peter edited *The Christian Messenger*.

In 1966-69 the Barkers lived at Nima where Peter was involved with GHAFES in Operation Help Nima.

In 1966 Peter was appointed Literature Secretary of the Christian Council of Ghana where he excelled in his passion for writing, editing and publishing books culminating in the founding of Asempa Publishers in 1968.

From 1970 to 1986 while serving at the Christian Council and managing Asempa Publishers, Peter contributed to the formation and development of Ghana Evangelism Committee/New Life for All in a variety of capacities.

In 1970-73 Peter facilitated the formation of the Evangelism Committee (later to become the Ghana Evangelism Committee) through a series of meetings and retreats which brought together leaders from The Christian Council of Ghana and Pentecostal denominations, Evangelical churches and Christian ministries to focus on the Great Commission.

In 1978 and 1979 Peter played a critical role in involving the churches of the Christian Council, Catholic Bishops Conference, major Pentecostal denominations and Christian organisations in three calls for prayer in times of national crisis.

In November 1984 Peter began researching the book 'Peoples, Languages and Religion in Northern Ghana' making two extended treks during the period to August 1985. The book was written and printed in 1986 after Peter's return to the UK.

In 1985 the family returned to the UK after having spent 22 years in the PCG ministry including the 18 years founding and managing Asempa Publishers.

Between 1996 and 2003 Peter researched and co-authored for Scripture Union the book *Changed by the Word*, an anniversary publication celebrating the work of Scripture Union in Ghana's schools. During this time he made three or four visits to Ghana.

From 1998 to 2001 Peter was assigned to the pastoral oversight of the Presbyterian Church of Ghana, Trinity Congregation—London.

Between 2005 and 2011 Peter made annual trips to Ghana to research a revision of his book, *Peoples, Languages and Religion in Northern Ghana*—trekking the north on public transport.

On 13 May 2016 Peter Barker was called home to Glory!

I remember Rev. Peter Barker well. He was present at many gatherings I attended as a student. And I once heard him preach in Twi (and with quotations from the Bible) with such dexterity as would have made the legendary Dr C. A. Akrofi jealous.

He has joined the saints who from their labours rest.

3

LEADERSHIP

Leadership should be seen as a call to influence and impact generations, present and future. The demands can be onerous, but the rewards are surely long-lasting.

PERSPECTIVES ON LEADERSHIP

I spoke at a half-day workshop on leadership for selected female senior executives from the Public Service of Ghana in August, 2016. Given the relevance of the subject, I propose sharing the highlights in this publication for general consumption. It is my hope that we shall all benefit from the fresh perspectives on leadership presented here. Remember that there is the leader in you.

LEADERSHIP IS DESTINY

There are no coincidencies in life. Look at things with that philosophy of life. Your outlook on leadership will then take on a new dimension. What you do with your leadership role and how you respond to its demands will determine your success and impact.

WHAT IS LEADERSHIP?

There are various definitions of leadership. Most focus on power, position and authority. But in reality, leadership is the ability to transform yourself and others for good. This means the ability to function effectively and make a difference. Leadership that has an enduring impact.

Dr John Edmund Haggai of the Haggai Institute for Advanced Leadership (Singapore and Hawaii) has a definition of leadership that is particularly revealing.

Dr Haggai defines leadership as:

> "The discipline of deliberately exerting special influence within a group to move it toward goals of beneficial permanence that fulfil the group's real needs."

I love this definition! I want us to look at aspects of this type of leadership.

Leadership is Stewardship

Leadership is that which influences for good and for generations. And true leaders are fully conscious of this huge responsibility. They view it as a call to which they respond with evangelical zeal.

Leadership is stewardship. What does this mean? It means that you will give an account for how you develop and nurture the people and resources under your control. Even if you do not believe in God (by the way the Bible calls such people fools) you will give an account to posterity for how you handled the responsibilities entrusted to you. Do not for once think that you are a Lord and Dame of all that you survey. What do you have that you did not receive?

Your position has been given to you as a trust. Manage the people and resources entrusted to your care faithfully, knowing that you are leaving imprints in the sands of time. If you are faithful in handling and building up people and institutions and investing resources judiciously, future generations will rise and mention your name with awe and respect because of the legacy you left behind. We have some examples of such people in the history of our Public Services. Mr A. L. Adu and Dr Robert Gardiner are only two examples, and their memories continue to evoke respect. It is required of stewards that they be found trustworthy.

Leadership is Discipline

Discipline in the use of resources. Leaders (and I am talking of leaders in the true sense of the word), do not misuse or misapply funds and property just because they think subordinates will be afraid to question them. Leadership means discipline in attitude to time. Leaders walk the talk. They set the right example. When they set a meeting time at 9 am, they are seated at 8.55 am. How would anyone dare to be late to such a meeting when they know that their leaders are disciplined and respect time?

One of the marks of a people with a future is discipline. Leaders use their time productively and their people and institutions become the better as a result. Without discipline an army will easily be defeated. Leaders who are disciplined gain credibility with their people. Leadership is discipline.

Leadership is Service

It is not a feudal relationship between Lords, Dames and Serfs, as in some of the stories we read about in history books. No. This is about humility. True leaders accept that they are who they are by God's grace alone. They do not lord it over their people.

The primary responsibility of a leader is to serve. Service that will lead to progress, development and the elimination of poverty, ignorance and all the things that keep people down. Service that will liberate and empower followers to achieve their full potential. Service that will serve as an example to all, especially to the young and up-and-coming. Leadership is service.

Leadership is Positive

It turns problems into opportunities for learning, unlearning and relearning.

Leadership does not spend precious time blaming circumstances and other people. It is courageous and does not hide behind bureaucracy, covering and shifting blame.

Leadership focuses on solutions. It does not take rocket science to find solutions to many of the problems that are sinking people into obscurity and needless hardships. Leadership is positive.

Leadership is Character

Leadership is integrity. It does not have two sets of rules, but maintains the same standard for all. That is character. In my view this is the single most important trait in leadership.

Character! The Akan language in Ghana has a word for it; "suban." Its roots go deep and denote wholeness of being. Truthfulness. Faithfulness. Transparency. No pollution. Dependable. Consistent. Each of these traits deserve full treatment, but that will be for another time.

That kind of leadership results in a good name that is better than riches. That leadership shows respect to others, and treats them well irrespective of their status, whether low or high, in society. This kind of leadership is mission oriented and does not waste time on frivolities and vainglory. It pursues the things that matter. It seeks to impact in people those good traits which no one can take away from them, and which will make such people truly fulfilled. Leadership is character.

Leaders Dream

Creativity is imagination applied. In other words, creativity is applied imagination. Leaders look at the present situation and dream of or imagine what could be to make life better for their people and then set goals to get to the desired destination. They see and present the big picture. As Dr Haggai puts it so beautifully, leadership begins when a vision emerges.

Leaders tell their people stories. Stories of how others have made it and how they and their people can also make it, and even do better. Stories of how obstacles have been overcome. They inspire their people that way. Their followers also start dreaming and imagining how things can be improved through their concerted efforts. There is no law against hope! Leaders dream, and their dreams lead their people to their desired havens. In this connection, I invite you to check out Martin Luther King, Jr's speech, "I have a dream."

> "I have a dream that one day this nation will rise up and live out the true meaning of its creed: 'We hold these truths to be self-evident: that all men are created equal'.
>
> I have a dream that one day on the red hills of Georgia the sons of former slaves and the sons of former slave owners will be able to sit down together at the table of brotherhood.
>
> I have a dream that one day even the state of Mississippi, a state sweltering with the heat of injustice, sweltering with the heat of oppression, will be transformed into an oasis of freedom and justice.
>
> I have a dream that my four little children will one day live in a nation where they will not be judged by the color of their skin but by the content of their character.
>
> I have a dream today.
>
> I have a dream that one day, down in Alabama, with its vicious racists, with its governor having

his lips dripping with the words of interposition and nullification; one day right there in Alabama, little black boys and black girls will be able to join hands with little white boys and white girls as sisters and brothers.

I have a dream today.

I have a dream that one day every valley shall be exalted, every hill and mountain shall be made low, the rough places will be made plain, and the crooked places will be made straight, and the glory of the Lord shall be revealed, and all flesh shall see it together.

This is our hope. This is the faith that I go back to the South with. With this faith we will be able to hew out of the mountain of despair a stone of hope. With this faith we will be able to transform the jangling discords of our nation into a beautiful symphony of brotherhood. With this faith we will be able to work together, to pray together, to struggle together, to go to jail together, to stand up for freedom together, knowing that we will be free one day.

This will be the day when all of God's children will be able to sing with a new meaning, 'My country, 'tis of thee, sweet land of liberty, of thee I sing. Land where my fathers died, land of the pilgrim's pride, from every mountainside, let freedom ring.'

And if America is to be a great nation this must become true. So let freedom ring from the prodigious hilltops of New Hampshire. Let freedom ring from the mighty mountains of New

York. Let freedom ring from the heightening Alleghenies of Pennsylvania!

Let freedom ring from the snowcapped Rockies of Colorado!

Let freedom ring from the curvaceous slopes of California!

But not only that; let freedom ring from Stone Mountain of Georgia!

Let freedom ring from Lookout Mountain of Tennessee!

Let freedom ring from every hill and molehill of Mississippi. From every mountainside, let freedom ring."

Dr Martin Luther King, Jr on a hot summer day in 1963. Washighton DC, USA.

Yes, Leaders dream.

Leadership Involves Good Role Modelling

Quality leadership is relationship oriented. It values people. Leadership, above all, takes an eternal perspective on everything. That is a huge responsibility! Wise leaders know that they are being watched and followed and great is that leader who deliberately makes good choices, knowing that the serious ones among his people will seek to replicate such behaviour and choices.

Leadership involves good role modelling.

4

PERSPECTIVES ON LEADERSHIP

At this juncture, we are going to look at a number of examples of the types of leaders we have been discussing. These are people who have created lasting, beneficial impact, and whose lives, I strongly recommend, we should aspire to follow.

SUSANNA WESLEY

Over the years I have heard and read about a woman called Susanna. By all accounts she was a remarkable person. What I just wrote is actually an understatement, judging from what I am going to be sharing about her. Susanna was born almost 350 years ago and lived for 73 years. She bore 19 (yes, 19) children, 9 of whom died before adulthood.

Needless to say she had no refrigerator, deep freezer, electric iron or any of the countless devices we now take for granted in our homes. Yet she ran her home very effectively and taught each of her children Latin and Greek. It is recorded that one son, John, was teaching Greek at Oxford by the age of 21. She ran a home school for all her children. History has it that she married a minister of the gospel who spent much of his time in debtors' prison because he did not know how to handle money! Managing of finances has always been an issue, hasn't it? Susanna refused to compromise her ideals and made sure that each of her children was brought up in the fear of the Lord Jesus Christ. As a result, her children turned out exceptionally well and impacted the world greatly. Susanna Wesley was the mother of Charles Wesley and John Wesley.

We should not underestimate the power of the influence of our lives on others. If we are wise, and have an eye for the future, we shall be circumspect about the way we live our lives. That is why I posited earlier that leadership involves good role modelling. We do not live in a vacuum.

According to some records, Sam (her husband) left her to raise the children alone for long periods of time. This was sometimes over something as simple as an argument. One of their children was crippled. Another couldn't talk until he was nearly six years old. Susanna herself was desperately sick most of her life. There was no money for food or anything. Debt plagued them. Sam was once thrown into debtors' prison because their debt was so high, which doubled their problems. Twice, the homes they lived in were burned to the ground, losing everything they owned. It was assumed that their church members did it because they were so mad at what Sam preached in the pulpit! Someone slit their cow's udders so they wouldn't have milk, killed their dog, and burned their flax field! When Susanna was young, she promised the Lord that for every hour she spent in entertainment, she would give to Him in prayer and in the Word. Taking care of the house and raising so many kids made this commitment nearly impossible to fulfil. She had no time for entertainment or long hours in prayer! She worked the gardens, milked the cow, schooled the children and managed the entire house herself. So, she decided to instead give the Lord two hours a day in prayer! She struggled to find a secret place to get away with Him. So she advised her children that when they saw her with her apron over her head, that meant she was in prayer and couldn't be disturbed. She was devoted to her walk with Christ, praying for her children and knowledge in the Word no matter how hard life was.

One of her daughters got pregnant out of wedlock and the man never married her. She was devastated, but remained steadfast in prayer for her daughter. In the end, she knew that one day her hard life would be over and she alone would stand before the throne of God and give an account of how she lived her life. We can be the best mum, wife, friend, person in the world and still have untold hardships. We need to take Susanna's example, flip our apron over our head and pray in the middle of it all.

Her sons' John and Charles were powerhouses for the glory of the Lord. John Wesley preached to nearly a million people in his day. At the age of 70 he delivered the gospel message of salvation to 32,000 people—without the use of a microphone! He brought revival everywhere he travelled!

His brother Charles wrote over 9,000 hymns, many of which we still sing today. Hidden behind the door of our homes, we want our children to find a mum who prays diligently— no matter how busy or how hard the circumstances.

Now, back to Susanna Wesley. Dr John Edmund Haggai asks a question which he then proceeds to answer. The question: Did Susanna Wesley influence the world? The answer: Yes. Through her son John, she contributed to these tremendous accomplishments, among others: . . . the abolition of the slave trade . . . the launching of the industrial revolution . . . the establishment of the YMCA and YWCA . . . the multiplication of public libraries . . . the creation of the Salvation Army . . . the creation of orphanages . . . the founding of the Methodist Church and all the great institutions born out of the Methodist Church worldwide.

In Ghana, as in many parts of the world, the influence of the Methodist Church has been immense. Pause to ask yourself: where would we be without the contribution of the Methodist Church? Imagine that Wesley College, Wesley Girls High School and Mfantsipim School had not been established? Certainly an unimaginable vacuum would have been created. I am not a Methodist, but I know about the work that the Susanna Wesley Mission Auxiliary (SUWMA) is doing in many parts of Ghana. The list could go on and on.

Susanna was said to be a time-management genius. In addition to the formidable list of household chores and other assignments she had to attend to, she made sure that she set aside one hour each week to pray for each of her children. This was a woman who had her eyes on the future, and who was sure in her conviction that the seeds she was sowing and watering would yield manifold harvests in years to come. Ask yourself, what legacy are you leaving? Who is going to remember you 10 or 20 or 30 years after you are gone? If they do remember you, how are they going to remember you? I hear that the epitaph on the tomb of Susanna Wesley reads: "The gnawing tooth of time will ultimately reduce this marble memorial to dust, but the influence of this devout mother will live as long as time lasts". What a testimony! How amazing! How inspiring!

JOYCE ASIBEY OF ABURI GIRLS

I am certain that we can all identify with leaders who have had continuing, lasting, permanent and beneficial impact on us.

Ghana saw off (in late 2015), a great leader with beneficial permanence, in the person of Mrs Joyce Asibey, the first Ghanaian Headmistress of Aburi Girls. Her death and the activities surrounding her funeral saw a genuine outpouring of grief and love at the same time.

Joyce Lucy Ama Korama Asibey (née Kyei) was born on January 31, 1931 at Agogo in the Ashanti Region of Ghana. Agogo is well known in Ghana for its educational institutions and the work of the Basel missionaries. The Basel Mission Girls School and Women's Training College (which my mother attended) are well known in Ghana. The Agogo Hospital is also well known for its ophthalmology services and Nursing Training School. The Presbyterian University College has a campus there.

Joyce was the first child of her parents, Mr T. E. Kyei, a teacher, and Madam Jane Akua Agyeiwaa, a farmer and baker. She had an early start to her education when she was sent to Achimota Primary School, from where she proceeded to Achimota School, the secondary department. She is said to have been an outstanding student, not just in academics but also in the sporting disciplines. From Achimota she was awarded the Asanteman Scholarship to study at Reading University in the United Kingdom. It is said that she was the first African female student at Reading.

She joined the teaching staff at Aburi Girls in 1957 right after her graduation from Reading University. She taught Geography, a subject she taught so well that it became the flagship subject for Aburi Girls. Her dedication and commitment to duty soon endeared her to both staff and students. Auntie Joyce, as she was affectionately called by all, became the first indigenous Headmistress of this famous school following the retirement of the last Scottish Head, Miss Irene Anderson in 1971. Before then she had served as Senior Housemistress and Assistant Headmistress under Miss Anderson. Auntie Joyce devoted her life and every ounce of her strength to build the school to become a pillar of scholarship, discipline and character.

She was noted for being firm. She was a strict disciplinarian who meted out disciplinary measures against all who went astray. Her motivation was to correct and set the offender on the right path. She was diminutive in appearance but behind it was a steely will to her convictions which would not allow her to bend the rules, even for the great and mighty in society. It was only after her death that many got to know of the lengths she went to, on the quiet, to seek and extend financial assistance to girls in the school whose education might have been truncated as a result of the inability of their parents to pay the bills. It was also reported that each year, she sent scouts to the little hamlets down the hills in the Aburi area to look for girls with promise from poor families who she then sponsored at this most-sought-after school.

She retired voluntarily in 1988 at age 58 after a period spanning more than three decades at Aburi Girls. After her departure from Aburi Girls, she joined the American Peace Corps, first as an Education Sector Specialist and then as Associate Director. This was from 1988 to 1991. Thereafter she settled down to a proper retirement and took up hobbies she had put on the back burner, as it were, due to the demands of her full-time job of looking after her girls at Aburi. She took particular delight in tending her vegetable garden at her home and also rearing snails. She also got actively involved in the lives of her girls.

It was always a joyous occasion whenever social activities brought her and her girls into contact. Groups of her girls from Aburi also took turns to visit her at home and to let her know how much she had impacted their lives for good. Her students never ceased to testify that her strength of character and self-control had helped to mould them into well-disciplined adults. She was a constant presence at Speech and Prize Giving Days and Annual Thanksgiving Services. She always received thunderous applause whenever she appeared at these functions.

Today, products of Aburi Girls are to be found in all spheres of life in Ghana and beyond. They, with one accord, mourned this great mother of their school, along with the rest of us, and all are unanimous that her influence on them has been continuing, lasting, permanent and beneficial. This is what leadership is about, to serve as a channel for lasting, eternal impact through generations.

CLARICE GARNETT (HOWORTH) OF WESLEY GIRLS HIGH SCHOOL

On a very cold, snowy and wintry February day in 2013, about one hundred old girls of Wesley Girls High School, Cape Coast, Ghana, descended on Rathmell, North Yorkshire in the United Kingdom. They came from Ghana, the United States, Europe and from different parts of the United Kingdom. Those from London made the four and a half hour journey in two coaches. They had come to mourn Mrs Clarice Howorth, popularly known as Miss Garnett or Garnie for short. Rathmell is a village in North Yorkshire. It is very English. The village had never seen anything like this before. And I doubt if it will witness another such scene again. The old girls came singing, and one of the songs they sang was the school hymn, "We build our school on thee, O Lord", to which they had added a fifth stanza all of their own eulogising their former Headmistress. Rathmell has a population of 269. The nearest town is called Settle. I know, because I went there to visit Garnie when she was alive, as did my wife Elioenai and my two older girls, Abena Okyerebea and Akua Adubea, on different occasions. I also know that every Headmistress of Wesley Girls after her, from Mrs Rosina Acheampong to Mrs Nancy Thompson to Mrs Betty Djokoto paid her regular visits during her lifetime.

For the next few pages I am going to be sharing part of the story of Clarice Garnett as I knew her. Let me make a disclosure right from the word go. My wife went to Wesley

Girls. All my four daughters (Abena Okyerebea, Akua Adubea, Eunice Awurabena and Afua Bentsiwa) also went there. A slighter higher number of nieces were there, not to mention my sisters-in-law who are also old students. The Akuapem Presbyterian in me had wanted my eldest daughter to attend Aburi Girls, a school we drive past every time we go to our country home at Abiriw. Any time we drove past Aburi Girls when my five adult children were young, I would brag about "Bepɔ so hann" (Light on a hill) and say "that is our school." I still do!

Then I dropped the bombshell one day. M'abena (Abena Okyerebea) is going to Aburi Girls after Ridge Church School! Almost immediately an army of five (Mummy and four girls, with my son Kofi remaining coolly neutral) bellowed, "but this is not fair, Daddy." I had to beat a quick retreat to avoid having a full blown rebellion on my hands. That is how come all four girls followed after their mother to Wesley Girls.

Who was Clarice Garnett (Howorth)?

Clarice Garnett (Howorth) of Wesley Girls High School.

Clarice Garnett, who died aged 86 at the end of January 2013, was born in Rathmell, a village near Settle in North Yorkshire, England. Her father was a builder. She was educated at Rathmell Primary School and Settle High School. She then went on to St Hugh's College, Oxford.

After graduating from Oxford, she taught science for a short period. Not long after she started teaching, she responded to a call by the Methodist Church and arrived in the then Gold Coast (now Ghana) in September 1950. She was posted straight to Wesley Girls High School, Cape

Coast, as a biology teacher. She plunged into her duties with all her heart. On the retirement of Miss Olive Compton as Headmistress in 1960, the mantle fell on Clarice and she became Headmistress, a position she held till she retired and went back home to Rathmell in 1981.

Every old girl of Wesley Girls who passed through her hands has her favourite story of Garnie. According to her old girls, she was one in a million. She had a soft, calm voice behind which was a lot of authority. She knew every girl by name and their character. It is reported that she travelled all over Ghana to interview girls who had passed the common entrance examination and qualified for Wesley Girls herself, and ensured that those who met the standards were admitted. The admissions were strictly on merit, and no one, absolutely no one, could influence the process. She was the resident warden, repairing watches, shoes, electric irons, dresses and whatever else needed attending to. These were all in addition to her duties as academic and administrative head.

A friend of ours who passed through her hands, and now a Consultant/Physician tells me that Garnie had the heart of a real mother. She cites the cases of a few girls who got pregnant halfway through their education. Garnie guided them and their parents after they had had to exit Wesley Girls. She then helped them to secure admission to other schools after they had their babies. This helped these girls to complete their secondary school education, and today some of these girls are in professions like law and pharmacy.

She applied her father's training as a builder in overseeing the construction of new classrooms, dormitories and other buildings. A lot of money was saved while quality work was done at the same time. She was a very good steward and epitomised what we saw earlier that leadership is stewardship.

The Methodist Church is very strong in the northern part of England. Soon after my arrival at the University of Bradford in September 1991 (as a mature student) to undertake the Bradford MBA, I asked the Wilkinson family of Hall Royd Methodist Church in nearby Shipley (where I first worshipped and incidentally made life-long friends) if they could locate Miss Garnett for me. I had heard so much about her and I knew she was somewhere in those parts. They made enquiries through the Methodist fraternity and soon after that I was given a telephone number. That started a very lovely relationship between the much-revered and beloved Garnie of Wesley Girls and me and subsequently with my family too. For a number of years after my return to Ghana, we kept in touch through correspondence. Of course, my wife Elioenai had been her student and she remembered her as a little girl on her entry to the school.

I visited Garnie in her home in Rathmell and met her husband Roland Howorth, who told me the circumstances leading to their marriage in old age. I was also very happy to meet Miss Barbara Bowman (popularly called Bowmie by her students) who was Miss Garnett's deputy at Wesley Girls. She lived in nearby Settle and she came to spend the time with me when I visited Miss Garnett at Rathmell with Mrs Vivienne Wilkinson of Hall Royd Methodist Church, Shipley. Everything in Garnie's home in Rathmell was Wesley Girls and Ghana, so to speak. Souvenirs from Ghana and mementos of Wesley Girls met you everywhere you turned in the house. There was even a Ghanaian traditional stool there. She radiated the love, care, concern, understanding spirit and discipline her students had been talking about all the time. This was someone who had touched many lives for good. She was a real mother who cared about the destiny of her girls.

In 1981, the year in which she left Ghana for good, Clarice Garnett was awarded the Order of the Volta by the Government of Ghana in appreciation of her great contribution to education in Ghana. Back in the United Kingdom, the Queen awarded her the MBE for her services to education.

On her return to England, she went back to her village, Rathmell. She took charge of the village shop, which included acting as postmaster and served in the church. She then married Roland Howorth, who predeceased her.

I met Roland during my visit to Rathmell, as I mentioned before. He was a very pleasant and well-mannered gentleman. He told me how they got to be husband and wife in their old ages.

THIS IS THE STORY

Roland Howorth had been a lecturer at the Department of Classics at the University of Ghana in the 1950s when Miss Garnett was at Wesley Girls. When he got married, Clarice was the Maid of Honour to his wife.

Roland and his wife left Ghana in 1958 to go back home to England and they maintained sporadic contact. Some time after Miss Garnett returned to England in 1981, she and her long-lost friends reconnected, though they did not meet in person. Then Mrs Roland Howorth fell ill and later went on admission in hospital and duty then drew Clarice to start paying regular visits to her old friend. Her friend died not long afterwards and Clarice kept in touch with Roland. After some time they decided that it would be a good idea to get married, and that is how come they did.

They were a lovely couple. Clarice teased Roland about how he was spending his time taking up a different course each year. At the time of my visit, he had just completed Advanced Level Physics!

Clarice Garnett was undoubtedly a great leader. She was a person who influenced her students for good and for eternity. She was a leader with permanent, beneficial impact.

She personified the motto of Wesley Girls, which is,
Live Pure,
Speak True,
Right Wrong,
Follow the King.

I end the feature on Clarice Garnett (Howorth) with a hymn written by Roland, Clarice's husband in about 2001 which speaks volumes about their Christian faith.

When Joseph and Mary so wearily wended
Their way from their cottage in Nazareth's street,
Then slept with the oxen in Bethlehem's stable,
And laid in a manger their Baby so sweet,
Enduring discomfort and squalor and hardship,
Compelled by a merciless tyrant's decree,
Few were there on earth who in such tribulation
God's greatness and goodness and glory could see.

God's glory we see in the sun, moon and planets,
In river and ocean, in mountain and plain,

In flowers and butterflies, forests and gardens,
In moors with their heather and fields full of grain.
But angels sang "Glory" when in great privation
Our Lord came in Bethlehem's manger to lie;
For His greatest glory's the glory of loving,
That led Him to suffer, that led Him to die.

Lord, give us Your glory, the glory of loving,
A love for all people, the great and the small,
For saints and for sinners, for friends and for strangers,
For black folk and white, like Your love for us all,
A love like Your own that for others is ready
To suffer great hardship if that should ensue;
You said that whenever we love other people
We also, in doing so show love to You.
©Roland Howorth.
Rathmell, North Yorkshire
Taken from *Craven Herald & Pioneer* of North Yorkshire.

S. T. AMPOFO OF OFORI PANIN SECONDARY SCHOOL

We are now going to look at another personality, this time still alive, who exemplifies the definition of leadership we have been using for our discourse.

You will recall that we have adopted Dr John Edmund Haggai's definition of leadership as being: "The discipline of deliberately exerting special influence within a group to move it toward goals of beneficial permanence that fulfil the group's real needs." We have demonstrated what this kind of leadership entails, and have seen some real life examples, who have so far been women, and great women at that.

I invite you to get to know Mr Samuel Twum Ampofo, about whom have I stated the following in the Acknowledgements section of each of my three earlier books, namely, *Stories to Warm Your Heart*, *Pearls of Wisdom* and *Nuggets for Victorious Living*: "I wish to place on record my gratitude to Mr S. T. Ampofo, my secondary school Headmaster at Ofori Panin. His sense of discipline, integrity and his desire to see his students become complete in all aspects of life, have contributed greatly in shaping me into what I am today."

About six years ago, I was seated next to my friend and classmate Ambassador Kwasi Baah-Boakye during his late mother's thanksgiving service at the Presbyterian Church of Ghana, Resurrection Congregation, Asiakwa, when he whispered to me: "Have you seen Oga?" Now to the two of us and any of our contemporaries from Ofori Panin Secondary School, Kukurantumi, Oga could only refer to our Headmaster, S. T. Ampofo. I responded in the negative and Kwasi then added, "there he is, playing the organ." I turned in excitement in the direction he pointed and, lo and behold, ST was at the organ and playing it in accompaniment to the singing by the choir and the packed congregation. What a joy it was to both of us as we saw each other. I followed him and his wife (since deceased) home after the service ended and ST could not hide his pleasure at seeing me and how far the grace of God had brought me.

S. T. Ampofo became Headmaster of Ofori Panin Secondary School, Kukurantumi, in September 1963, the same year I entered the school as a 12-year-old Form One boy. Opass, as the school is popularly known, was then in its third year of existence, having been established by

Ghana's first President, Dr Kwame Nkrumah, as one of the Ghana Educational Trust schools in 1961. Schools in that category include Swedru, Tema, Mfantsiman, Mpraeso, Yaa Asantewaa and Accra Girls.

Born at Asiakwa, in Ghana, on August 1, 1925, S. T. Ampofo trained as a teacher at the Presbyterian Training College, Akropong Akuapem and continued at the Seminary there to become a Catechist as well. He graduated with an honours degree in history from the then University College of the Gold Coast in 1957 after which he taught at Abetifi Training College before being appointed Assistant Headmaster at Swedru Secondary School, the first Ghana Educational Trust School, in 1960.

It was from Swedru that ST was appointed Headmaster of Ofori Panin in 1963. He replaced Kwame Adwedaa, the first Headmaster, who was reassigned to the newly established Ghana Atomic Energy Commission as one of the pioneering scientists.

Being only in its third year of existence, Ofori Panin Secondary School was at that time a small school.

ST however proved himself to be a visionary. Well has it been said that leadership begins when a vision emerges. He was determined to make his students believe in themselves. He wanted them to feel prepared and adequate to rub shoulders with the best students from the then older and established schools. Above all, he wanted his students to become future leaders. I remember the "Open House" he held with us students, young as we were, on the school crest and motto, "Dwen na som", meaning Think and Serve. He was persuaded that he had a mission to get us to think and serve in the truest sense by instilling in us a high sense of discipline and integrity based on strong Christian foundations.

Whether by coincidence or design, the earliest crop of teachers were truly brilliant and dedicated. ST pulled them along on his mission. Robert Addo-Fening (later Professor at the University of Ghana and one of Ghana's foremost historians), V. B. Freeman (great English teacher and later Headmaster of Accra Academy), K. Twum-Danso (another wonderful English teacher who became Headmaster after ST), W. E. Amoah (Senior Housemaster who joined from Presec, Odumase), Gabriel Etu (Assistant Headmaster), J. B. Ofosu (Mathematics), Boniface Adjei (later Headmaster at New Juaben) and Susan Asomaning (American wife of Dr E. J. A. Asomaning, Director of the nearby Cocoa Research Institute of Ghana at New Tafo) are some of the names that readily come to mind.

Somehow he always managed to get a regular stream of US Peace Corps and Canadian volunteers to teach at the school. This may have had something to do with the environment, as the Kukurantumi and Tafo area (with the Cocoa Research Institute of Ghana) is really pristine, not to mention the intellectual firepower concentrated in that corridor.

S. T. was Chaplain, Music Director, Sports Coach and Headmaster combined

Those were the days before television. Radio reigned supreme. ST must have been an avid listener of radio and he made sure that he briefed us on the latest developments in the world as reported by the BBC World Service in particular. I remember the morning he announced that Dr

Albert Schweitzer had died. I had not heard of him before then. He went on to tell us about his great medical and humanitarian work among lepers in Central Africa. He was concerned that we should learn from the lives of pacesetters. To this end, he invited credentialed leaders to the school to speak to us on Speech and Prize Giving Days as well as on other occasions. He appeared to have earned the respect of all the eminent people he invited because not once (so far as I could tell) did any of them ever turn down an invitation to visit us and speak to us.

Eminent personalities like Mr William Ofori Atta (Paa Willie), Prof. K. Twum-Barima, Prof. Samuel Sey, Mr T. A. Osae of Prempeh College and Mr A. A. Beeko of Presec (later to become Moderator of the Presbyterian Church of Ghana), were regular visitors to the school. He arranged for the British Council to send an educational van to the school each term to screen Shakespeare and Charles Dickens classics we were treating. I still remember *Great Expectations* and characters like Pip and Estella.

S. T. Ampofo loved sports. With his support and the presence of W. E. Amoah as Sports Coach, sports prospered at Opass. He believed in the combination of a sound mind and a sound body. The school produced championship teams in hockey, football, athletics and table tennis, with perhaps the most famous athlete of our days being Hilda Kwabua. Hilda gained national prominence by setting a national record in the 880 yards.

Because the school was so new, Mr Ampofo wore many hats. He was an innovator, whose admission policy ensured that there were students from most parts of Ghana, even if the greater proportion came from the Eastern Region because of proximity. In our time, we even had two students from Kenya on Ghana Government scholarship.

He knew every student by name and knew which town or village they hailed from. He also knew most parents. ST admonished us to live lives of honesty, integrity and transparency. Before examinations, he always told us that it was better to fail honourably than to pass dishonourably. At morning assembly, you could not help observing his demeanour when we sang hymns. You could tell that he was singing with meaning and conviction. His students, and those who followed after he left, are to be found in all spheres of life in both Ghana and abroad. From the Supreme Court of Ghana through to academia, to the military, police and other security services, in agriculture, medicine and engineering, teaching, the civil service, the diplomatic service, banking and finance, Parliament and to the executive arm of Government.

We are all testimony to the fruit of his labour and to the seeds he planted, and encouraged others to plant, leading us to live the motto, "Dwen na Som", or Think and Serve. ST and his wife, Margaret Lillian, got married in 1951. They have three daughters, one of who (Nancy, an Opassian), is a nationally known lawyer and immediate past National Treasurer of the Ghana Bar Association. Sadly, his wife passed away in October, 2014.

I shall end with what must certainly be one of S. T. Ampofo's favourite scripture passages, judging by the number of times I heard him quote it when I was his student:

"Search me, O God, and know my heart: Try me, and know my thoughts: And see if there be any wicked way in me, And lead me in the way everlasting" (Ps 139:23-24 KJV).

Let me say that this passage of scripture has had, and continues to have, a profound impact on me as a result.

May all who call themselves leaders or aspire to be such, exhibit these values which have permanent, beneficial impact on their followers. We need such leaders in Ghana and Africa.

REXFORD AYEH DARKO OF MECHANICAL LLOYD FAME

I am sure that each of us can point to one or two people whose lives and contributions to society have influenced us in some way, whether we knew them personally or by reputation. In my hometown of Abiriw, on the Akuapem ridge, one person whose name is etched in the minds of people, old or young, is the late Rexford Ayeh Darko, popularly referred to as Yaw Barima or Yaw Anye, of Mechanical Lloyd fame. His father was from Akropong and his mother from Abiriw. He died in 1977 and yet I doubt if anyone at Abiriw or Akropong has not heard of him. I am referring to people who were born long after he died. He was a philanthropist who helped set up a lot of people. His crowning achievement, so far as the people of Abiriw are concerned, is the fact that he single-handedly constructed what is still one of the best chapels for the Presbyterian Church of Ghana there. He was on a trip to the then West

Germany to finalise the purchase of bells for the church tower when he died suddenly.

He was mourned by the people of Abiriw, Akropong and the whole of Okuapeman in a most moving way. His influence persists to this day. So, we should each be asking ourselves, "What kind of influence am I having on the people around me?"

WHAT COULD BE THE MOTIVATION?

The reactions I keep receiving whenever I share the stories of some of the people being discussed attest to the fact that our society recognises the need for the right type of leader in all spheres. The examples we have seen from the lives of Susanna Wesley, Joyce Asibey, Clarice Garnett and S. T. Ampofo have demonstrated beyond all doubt that leadership is about enduring, permanent and beneficial impact. Those who claim, or aspire, to be leaders in our time need a fundamental rethink of what it is that leadership entails and how they should go about living out that role. The kind of leadership under discussion does not come about by happenstance. "Once is happenstance, twice is coincidence, the third time is enemy action," so wrote Ian Fleming in *Goldfinger*.

WHAT COULD THE MOTIVATION BE? I ASK AGAIN

There is an evangelical zeal about what we are driving at. There is something methodical about it. There is a sense of destiny about it.

It is a recognition and acceptance of a call to shape and influence lives. This is evident from the examination of the four personalities we discussed.

"Lives of great men all remind us, we can make our lives sublime; and departing, leave behind us, footprints on the sands of time." — Henry Wadsworth Longfellow

Leadership means planting seeds that would blossom into great trees long after the leaders are gone. The leader knows for sure that he may not live to enjoy the fruit of his labour. That however, does not stop him from taking the long-term view, making sacrifices and decisions and taking stands that could prove unpopular in the short term. Leaders in this mould seek to improve on themselves constantly so that they can be better at what they are doing. This involves self-development, and all development is self-development.

LEADERSHIP IS SELF-DEVELOPMENT

Indeed leaders seek to improve on themselves constantly so they can be better at what they are doing, and this involves self-development.

Such an approach involves challenging existing mindsets. It means that leaders who understand their calling do not follow patterns blindly without seeking to understand the what, the why, the how and the when of such practices.

It also involves enlarging your horizon. One good way of doing this is to read good books, especially biographies and autobiographies of achievers. Having eyes that not only look, but eyes (and ears) that see and note the deep things that are hidden from those who only look casually. By the way, if we had eyes that really see, we would not be sitting at the river estuary and sending out SOS messages that we are thirsting! We would see and appreciate the numerous blessings God has bestowed on us, add value to them and never ever again behave like paupers. It means listening to different viewpoints and making the right deductions.

YES, WHAT COULD THE MOTIVATION BE?

We need to keep asking this question and seeking answers in order to understand the dynamics of true leadership.

At times, leadership means networking and learning from others.

It certainly means recording your observations and picking learning points from them. Such leadership takes notes all the time. It means writing it down, as you never know when that idea will disappear and not come back to you again.

> "Then the LORD answered me and said: 'Write the vision And make it plain on tablets, That he may run who reads it'" (Hab 2:2 NKJV).

Dr Paul A. Acquah, Governor of the Bank of Ghana from 2001 to 2009, was very effective in doing this. He had an incisive mind, which nevertheless did not prevent him from listening to different viewpoints and seeking answers to the pointed questions he could ask. At the end of deliberations at the top executive level, I never stopped admiring the way he summarised discussions and brought out the salient matters that needed to be worked on. He did not accept that things should be done in a certain way merely because that was how they had always been done. You needed to convince him with rational arguments. And you had better be prepared if attending a meeting presided over by him.

ADDITIONAL STATEMENTS ABOUT WHAT LEADERSHIP IS ABOUT. MAKE IT SIMPLE

Do not complicate matters.

True leaders have a way of breaking down complex issues into simple blocks, making ideas understandable to their people. They do not preach theories which their followers cannot identify with or conceptualise. I refer to Paul A. Acquah again. He would interrupt you gently if you started going off tangent with pointless theories and arguments with the words, 'do not complicate matters!' Oh, how we sometimes used to have good laughs over some issues which were nowhere complicated but which some people tried to make so.

I would remind him that Confucius made the same point about making things simple. By the way, this was someone who never signed any letter or document with his title 'Dr' because he held the view that it was your contribution that mattered, not the letters before or after your name. He held degrees from the University of Ghana, Yale University and the University of Pennsylvania (The Wharton School). Contrast that with the clamour for titles and fake doctorate degrees by so many people in our society. As we say in Akan, "ahene pa nkasa" meaning the genuine gem does not need to speak for others to know its worth.

The Bible has something to say about this:
"This is all that I have learnt: God made us plain and simple, but we have made ourselves very complicated" (Eccl 7:29 GNB).

THE TYPE OF LEADERSHIP WE HAVE BEEN DISCUSSING DOES NOT GIVE UP

Not on institutions.

Not on family.

Not on people.

Not on country.

Not on its principles.

It does not lose sight of its vision.

Remember that we are, at this stage, making additional statements as to what leadership entails.

Leadership is commitment. An unalloyed commitment to people and their well-being. Leadership is not for the sake of the leader.

Leadership is special influence. An influence that is earned, not forced.

Leadership inspires and fosters unity and cohesion. Not factionalism.

Leaders watch what they say. They know that the tongue is an uncontrollable fire. They are good people, who foster unity and goodwill. Good people will be remembered as a blessing, but the wicked will soon be forgotten, the Bible says in Proverbs 10:7.

What Ghana (and Africa) needs are leaders who understand that leadership is more than position, power and authority.

We need leadership which influences for lasting impact.

Leadership characterised by a sense of stewardship, integrity, humility, character, discipline, positivity, good role modelling, service and an eternal perspective.

As Ken Blanchard puts it: "The key to successful leadership today is influence, not authority".

EPHRAIM (OWURA) AMU'S RALLYING CRY

I shall give the final word to Ephraim Amu (Owura Amu) and I start by quoting the words of his famous song which is (or should be) known by everyone in Ghana. It is the alternative national anthem, known by everyone who has gone through the basic educational system in Ghana.

It is a rallying cry to Ghanaians to cherish their country. It sits very well with what we have been sharing on leadership.

> [1]Yɛn ara asaase ni;
> Ɛyɛ abooden de ma yɛn,
> Mogya a nananom hwie gui;
> Nya de too hɔ maa yɛn,
> Adu me ne wo nso so,
> Sɛ yɛbɛyɛ bi atoa so.
> Nimdeɛ ntraso, nkoto-kranne;
> Ne apɛ sɛ menkominya,
> Adi yɛn bra mu dɛm,
> ma yɛn asase ho dɔ atom' sɛɛ.

> *Chorus 2x:*
> Ɔman no, sɛ ɛbɛyɛ yie o!
> Ɔman no, sɛ ɛrenyɛ yie o!
> Ɛyɛ nsɛnnahɔ sɛ, ɔmanfo bra na ɛkyerɛ.

---

[1] https://abibitumikasa.com/forums/showthread.php/37621-Y%ce%b5n-Ara-Asase-Ni-(De-facto-National-Anthem-of-Ghana)-with-Translation

English translation:
This is our own native land;
That is a valuable thing to us,
Acquired through the blood our ancestors shed
for us;
It is now our turn to continue what our ancestors
started,
Know-it-all behaviour, cheating and selfishness;
Has scarred our character and diminished our
affection for our land.

Chorus 2x:
Whether or not this nation prospers!
Clearly depends on the character of the citizens
of the nation.

May all who call themselves leaders, and those aspiring to be, make time to reflect on these words and evaluate themselves against them. Are they leaders? Or shall we call them something else?

Are you a leader?
The second stanza of Owura Amu's song says:

Nhoma nimdeɛ huhugyan, Anaa adenya ara kwa;
Ne ɔbrakyew de ɛsɛe, ɔman na ɛbɔ no ahohora;
Asoɔmmerɛ ne obu pa, yɔnko yiyɛdi pɛ daa,
Ahofama ntetekwaam' ma onipa biara yiyɛdi;
Ɛnonom na ɛde asomdwee ne nkɔso pa brɛ ɔman.

Chorus 2x:
Ɔman no, sɛ ɛbɛyɛ yie o!
Ɔman no, sɛ ɛrenyɛ yie o!
Ɛyɛ nsɛnnahɔ sɛ, ɔmanfo bra na ɛkyerɛ.

In English:
Bragging of educational achievements;
Or useless greed for material things,
And bad lifestyles are destroying our nation,
and disgracing it.
Obedience and respect;
Caring for the welfare of one another every day,
Selflessness in the traditional way;
Ensures each person's welfare,
That is what will bring peace
and prosperity to our nation.

Chorus 2x:
Whether or not this nation prospers!
Clearly depends on the character of the citizens
of the nation.

Before I draw the curtain down on this most important topic of leadership, let me take you to my book, *Stories to Warm Your Heart* (Step Publishers, 2016) in which I devote a chapter to Owura Amu, and share one of the lessons from his life, as I saw it.

Leadership comes with a cost, and it can be heavy. Are you prepared to pay the price? A dear friend of mine, laments the craze and attraction for leadership positions in our society. He points out, rather sadly, that the motivation seems to be for the benefits and associated rewards, and not one of service nor of giving an account in most cases. Let us pray that many of us will have a better understanding of leadership so that we live up to the real demands of the role.

"NO CROSS, NO CROWN"

It has been said that life is not a bed of roses. This somehow becomes more real when we have set goals for ourselves. Sometimes it appears as if all the powers of the universe are against us, determined to stop us from achieving our goals. We should never give up, and should instead keep reminding ourselves of what we set out to do in the first place and keep working towards it. We need to have the strength of mind and resolve to face any opposition and obstacle and practise the discipline needed, whether in the area of time management, use of money or upholding of our cherished values. *"Momma yɛnkɔso mforo"* (let us continue to climb); Owura Amu continues to encourage us in his song by that title. *"Koko n'atifi da so wɔ akyirikyiri. . . yeguso foro nso yɛnya mmɛn atifi ee . . ."* (the summit is still some way off, we are nevertheless still climbing). *"Momma yɛnkɔso mforo"*. Let us continue climbing, and not give up. "So let's not get tired of doing what is good. At just the right time we will reap a harvest of blessing if we don't give up" (Gal 6:9 NLT). Remember, "no cross, no crown."

Excerpted from *Stories to Warm Your Heart*.

POSTSCRIPT TO PERSPECTIVES ON LEADERSHIP

A friend of mine based in the United States, Dr Stephen Ampofo, sent me a note after reading some of my earlier writings on leadership which encapsulates some of the key features of the subject we have been discussing.

"Thank you, Kofi. You have brought the series of the all-inspiring leadership series to an end on a good note by highlighting lessons learnt from the life and songs written by Owura Amu. I like reading about Dr Ephraim Amu and his feats in life and I find his life intriguing and challenging. As a student at the middle boarding school at Peki, Amu approached his music teacher to train on the organ and in return worked on the teacher's farm. When growing up and I learnt that my uncle Dr Oku Ampofo used to walk all the way from his Amanase (near Suhum) home carrying his chop box some 90 miles to school at Anum (Presbyterian Middle Boarding School), I was baffled by the strength of his determination to succeed. Like some of the men of that generation who desired to improve on their lot, Amu is also reported to have walked even longer distances; 150 miles from Peki to Abetifi carrying his box on his head to school when he gained admission to the Abetifi Seminary. Back to his former school at Peki as a teacher, Amu purchased an organ for his students from Koforidua but he arrived at Frankadua late and found no motor vehicle to continue the journey. He decided to walk the 18 miles journey overnight carrying the organ on his head to arrive at Peki in the morning so his students could benefit from his training. Later, while teaching agriculture at Akropong PTC he did the unthinkable when he demonstrated his leadership by carrying night soil to manure the school farm when his students hesitated in doing so on his instruction because they found it demeaning for the educated person to carry human excreta. And, contrary to the notion among the elites of his days in regard to the African culture, Owura Amu decided to wear the native cloth to church with pride much to the displeasure of his bosses with the dire consequence of being forced to forfeit pursuing his goal to be ordained as a minister of the gospel, being content to carry out God's work at the catechist level. These are but a few qualities that shaped him into the effective leader he was. Amu was a trailblazer. His determination and courage to stand tall in the face of incredible odds should be an example for us and posterity to follow, and the story told and read in our schools for character building and national patriotism. Thanks, Kofi, for feeding us with the unwritten aspects of Owura Amu's life in your books."

By the way, the Dr Oku Ampofo referred to progressed from an Akuapem "akuraa" (hamlet) called Amanase through Anum Presbyterian Boarding School to Mfantsipim and ended up at the prestigious University of Edinburgh Medical School to become one of the most renowned doctors in Ghana when I was a child. I remember my mother taking me to him at his clinic at Mampong. He was the brain behind the establishment of the Centre for Scientific Research into Plant Medicine at Mampong Akuapem, next door to the Tetteh Quarshie Memorial Hospital.

May we take inspiration from the lives of Owura Amu and all the others whose lives we have looked at.

No cross, no crown.

5

THE DISCIPLINE
OF WORK

The true leader understands the place and value of work and uses it as a powerful mentoring tool.

WORK IS PART OF THE LEADERSHIP JOURNEY

Please come along with me to look at some aspects of what I call the discipline of work. A common thread running through our just-ended discussion on leadership and the few practical examples given is work, even if not stated in so many words. Leadership involves work. Leadership is work. To start with, let us be clear about what work is.

WHAT IS WORK?

The *Oxford English Dictionary* has a good definition, in my view. "Work," it says, "is the application of mental or physical effort for a purpose." There is the use of energy, whether mental or physical. Whether you are working, as an employee or self-employed or whether you are yet to fall into any of those categories, an understanding of the discipline of work is important. Why work?

We shall attempt an answer to the question and follow up with a review of aspects of what constitute the discipline of work in the next few pages.

WHY WORK?

I want to make it clear, right from the word go, that we are dealing with a discipline. Discipline means order, structure and purpose. It is something you commit to, whether you feel like it or not. You pursue a discipline because you know that out of it will come something good.

So back to our question, why work?

First, we work in order to earn a living. This means that you do not become a parasite on others. Unless you are prevented from working by reason of ill health, infirmity or some other justifiable reason, it is imperative that you find something to do. You will always find something to do to earn a living if only you are not "choosy" and feel that some things are beneath you. Am I sounding controversial?

Second, we work in order to provide for our needs and those of others, especially our families and others who may need our help. This flows naturally from the first reason we gave.

Third, we work for our self-esteem. There is nothing as humiliating as asking an able-bodied young person what he or she does for a living and for him or her to say that they are not doing anything. Note that I did not say unemployed. The problem is that a lot of people are looking for traditional, office jobs which may be in short supply while with a little imagination they could start something little to solve the problems, and meet the needs, of others. And in doing so they will be meeting their need to earn a living and be a channel of blessing to others. But that is a completely different subject for another time. My answer to the question posed therefore is that work is a part of human existence.

Listen to what the Apostle Paul had to say:

> "While we were with you, we used to say to you, 'Whoever refuses to work is not allowed to eat'" (2 Thess 3:10 GNB).

WHAT KIND OF ATTITUDE SHOULD I BRING TO MY WORK?

I have to say that for some of us, we look at work as something to be endured. Work is a burden, drudgery and in some extreme cases some workers regard what they are doing as slave labour or in common parlance in Ghana some time back, "by day."

If work is for the reasons we looked at earlier, namely to earn a living, to provide for our needs and for our self-esteem, then we ought to approach it with expectation and enthusiasm. It is something we should look forward to as we get up from bed each day, knowing that we are working for good reasons. On the other side of the spectrum, there are others also who approach work as if that is all there is in the world, and in the process treat people anyhow and sacrifice relationships. What we are seeking to do is to bring out the right balance between these two extremes so that work becomes a meaningful, enjoyable, and profitable experience.

WORK IS CENTRAL TO OUR LIVES

Some people report to work to mark time. They put in the barest minimum to avoid the sack or other disciplinary action. Beyond that they are indifferent to what they are doing. This leads to poor quality and output. Needless to say, such an attitude results in laziness. Worse still, there is constant grumbling and complaining among such people.

Such behaviour is counterproductive and can be fatal to our leading fulfilled lives. This is because work is central to our lives, and we ignore that truth at our peril. Based on my own experience of being associated with the workplace for more than 40 years (though I am now retired from full-time work), I can say without fear of contradiction that many workers spend up to about 16 hours on average a day away from home for work-related reasons. That is, if you factor in commute time. If you add the time spent sleeping, you will realise that most of your waking hours are, or should be, spent working or doing things related to work. What better way to find meaning and satisfaction in what you are doing than by having the right understanding of the place of work in our lives? When we do, we shall find ourselves showing loyalty to our bosses and institutions and, if we are working for ourselves, getting more out of what we are doing.

And talking of working for ourselves, I do not want us to lose sight of the invaluable and unquantifiable work that some of our mothers have been doing in being at home (away from the formal workplace setting) taking care of our children and grandchildren. The principles we are discussing apply to them equally, and sometimes even more so, as without their devotion their families would not be able to cope. If you go back to read the earlier passages on Susanna Wesley under the Leadership series, you will see the generational impact that this full-time mother has had on the world, all because she took her work as a mother seriously.

GOD HIMSELF IS A WORKER

For those of us who are people of faith, we believe that God is a worker. He was a worker in creation. He had to work, and then rest on the seventh day.

Some people ignore this to their peril. Rest and recreation are important. Some of us have become so preoccupied with work that it is all that matters. Work. Work. Work. Work has become a form of idolatry. A religion. Many years ago, I heard the story of an executive so obsessed with his "empire" that his wife had to invade his office (literally) one night with his daughter so that they could get help with the child's homework. Interestingly enough, he lost control over that empire he thought was his bona fide property a few years after that. I have heard stories of people who on their deathbeds wished they had spent more time with their families. But alas, it was too late.

Having made the preceding observation, we should still remember that work is central to our lives. There should therefore be no room for loafing and giving of excuses for not doing what is expected of us. We also believe that God has created us in His image. The way we work will therefore show how much we have allowed the image of God to develop in us. We shall be looking at practical manifestations of how we should conduct ourselves as far as work is concerned on the next few pages before we draw the curtain down on this series.

WHAT WE DO MATTERS TO GOD

Work is dignifying and brings a sense of purpose to our lives. It makes us complete.

There are habits and behaviours that should be the hallmark of our work, if we are to be true to ourselves, our bosses and to our God.

There should be no distinction between the secular and the sacred if we believe that what we do matters to God. After all is said and done, our beliefs should affect our behaviour. Whether you are a trader, teacher, cleaner, painter, nurse, electrician, doctor, apprentice, driver, hairdresser or whatever you are doing, there should be faithfulness in every aspect of the work you are engaged in. Faithfulness in little things makes all the difference and leads to bigger opportunities. Whether you are an employee or trainee, please do not shortchange your employer or boss. Do not steal his or her time. And do not entice your employer's customers away from the business to a rival one set up by you or someone else while you are still with that business. It is the height of treachery and disloyalty. In any event, if your employer is so bad, why are you still in his or her employment? Why not leave, instead of staying put to destroy the hands that feed you?

> "Well, whatever you do, whether you eat or drink,
> do it all for God's glory" (1 Cor 10:31 GNB).

WORK AS UNTO THE LORD

This means going about your duties with enthusiasm, wholeheartedly and with energy. Your concern is to give of your best, and not preoccupied with whether everyone else is matching your contribution level. You know that you are responsible to God, ultimately, and He sees and knows the truth. It is His approval that matters. This makes a lot of difference and leads to satisfied customers and repeat business as well as a very fulfilled you. There are service providers I have used for years because I can vouch for their dependability and responsiveness. There are some others however, especially electricians, plumbers and painters I avoid like the plague because of their bad track record with me. It seems to me that the main preoccupation of some of these artisans is to milk you and not to provide quality service. They are out to cheat by adopting shortcuts and using inferior materials if you let down your guard for a moment.

On the positive side let me give just one example of a tailoring shop on Asafoatse Nettey Road in Accra manned by two brothers (the Laryea brothers @Chez Pierre a la mode) whose services I used from 1973 (while still at university) till 2015, a period spanning over 40 years. I used them, not because of the absence of equally good competition closer to me but because they served me and their other customers

94

with unparalleled dedication. Following the passing away of, first, the older brother about 20 years ago, followed by the younger one in 2015, I made a decision to use some tailors nearer my residential area.

Understanding the discipline of work means a determination to do whatever you are doing well. It means working as unto God. And that involves energy, enthusiasm, and wholeheartedness.

> "Work willingly at whatever you do, as though you were working for the Lord rather than for people" (Col 3:23 NLT).

SEE WORK AS A CALLING

If you see work as divine, as one of my spiritual leaders put it on one occasion, you will exhibit certain tendencies in addition to what we have already seen.

You will seek to excel in all you do. Your handiwork and output will make you stand out from the crowd. As you approach every assignment, you will do a self-examination aimed at ensuring that you are being true to yourself, employers, colleagues and ultimately to your God.

These are some of the questions you should be asking yourself constantly in that self-examination: Am I devoting my best attention to the work at hand? Am I doing my work with honesty or is there an ulterior, selfish motive I need to get rid of? Is my heart in what I am doing? Will my contribution at work add value to others, be they institutions or individuals? Can others vouch for my faithfulness? Do I do my work for the glory of God? Does my work ethic encourage others to seek to become excellent and enthusiastic about their work? Imagine what productive and happy homes, institutions and countries we would have if we saw work as a discipline and a complete ministry. May God help us all to accept and practise the Discipline of Work.

"Through hard work, perseverance and a faith in God, you can live your dreams." —Ben Carson

"Do you see a man who excels in his work? He will stand before kings; He will not stand before unknown men" (Prov 22:29 NKJV).

Interacting with Prince Kofi Amoabeng (Board Chairman) and the Hon Gifty Twum-Ampofo, MP at OPASS Speech Day

A section of the audience at the 55th Annual Speech and Prize Giving Day at Ofori Panin Senior High School (OPASS)

With S. T. Ampofo (left) the legendary former headmaster of OPASS after the 55th Speech and Prize Giving Day

Delivering the keynote address at OPASS

The legendary Mrs Joyce Asibey (right) of Aburi Girls pictured after a function at Aburi Girls

My chaplain and friend Rev. Dr G. O. Kwapong. Former Chairperson, Akuapem Presbytery of the Presbyterian Church of Ghana

Auntie Joyce Asibey (middle) with Rosina Osae-Quansah (left) and another old girl at a function at Aburi Girls.

Participants at the City of London programme. The author is left on the front row

London Business School. The author is seated on the extreme right

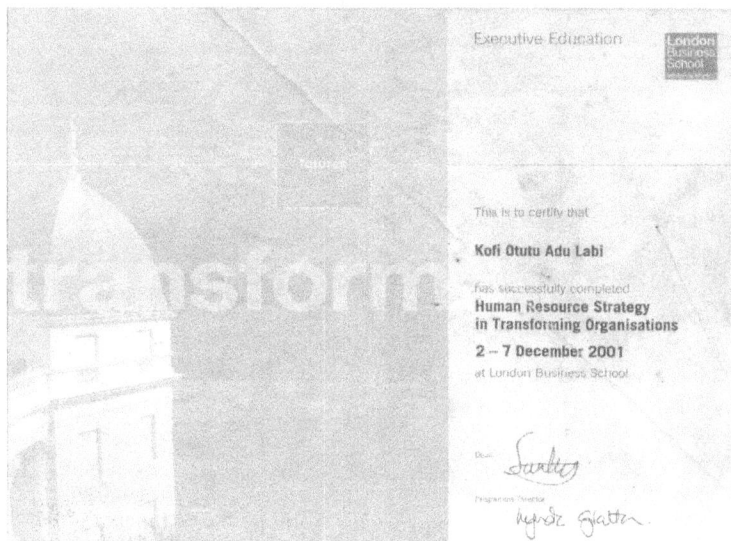

Mrs Esther Afua Ocloo of Nkulenu Industries

The original administration building at the Cocoa Research Institute of Ghana, Tafo

Visiting a cocoa farm at the Cocoa Research Institute of Ghana, Tafo, with daughter Afua and wife Elioenai

*Rt Rev. Prof. Cephas Omenyo, Moderator on a visit to the Victory
Congregation of the PCG, Fafraha*

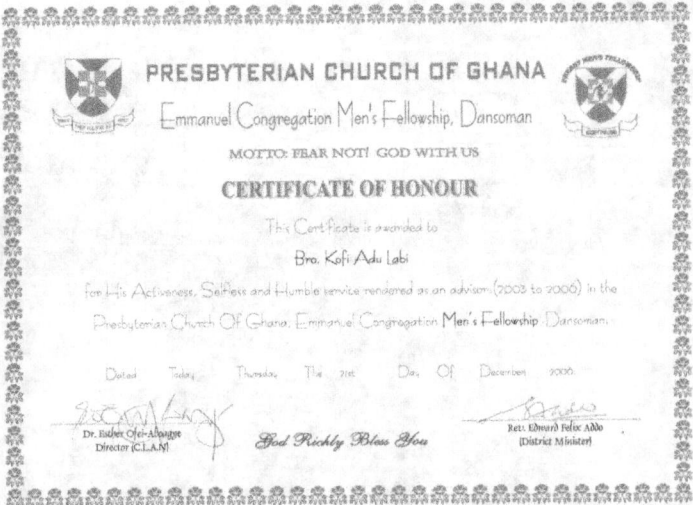

PRESBYTERIAN CHURCH OF GHANA

Emmanuel Congregation Men's Fellowship, Dansoman

MOTTO: FEAR NOT! GOD WITH US

CERTIFICATE OF HONOUR

This Certificate is awarded to

Bro. Kofi Adu Labi

for His Activeness, Selfless and Humble service rendered as an advisor (2003 to 2006) in the
Presbyterian Church Of Ghana, Emmanuel Congregation Men's Fellowship, Dansoman.

Dated Today Thursday The 21st Day Of December 2006

Dr. Esther Ofei-Aboagye
Director (C.L.A.N)

God Richly Bless You

Rett. Edward Felix Addo
(District Minister)

*From Dansoman Emmanual Congregation of the PCG,
my mother church*

Dr Ama Boohene-Andah speaking at the Victory Business and Fair 2016

Cranfield School of Management. The author is standing third from the right

At a capital markets conference for Africa and the Middle East. The author is second from the left on the front row

Speaking at the Calvary Congregation of the PCG at Abiriw in June 2017 on the 10th anniversary of my mother's passing. Left to Right: me, Robert Adu-Mante (Senior Presbyter and cousin), sisters Akua, Ohenewa, Akosua, Amma and brothers Kwabena and Yaw.

Mrs Clarice Howorth (Garnett) of Wesley Girls

My mother, Yaa Okyerebea Adu Labi

6

MEMORIES, MEMORIES AND MORE MEMORIES

W e are building memories and writing our life stories with each passing day. It is sobering to realise that someone somewhere may benefit from your example and experience. Be careful how you write your script.

WHEN DR JAMES GIBBS WROTE FROM BRISTOL, ENGLAND

Dr James Gibbs is an academic, researcher, literary editor and arts critic. He has written a monograph on the Nobel Laureate Wole Soyinka for Macmillan (1986). I want to encourage you to google <James Gibbs Wole Soyinka> for publications that include articles on Soyinka and Road Safety, on Soyinka's Plays in Production and on Soyinka as an autobiographer. The *Portrait of the Artist as a Young Traveller* written by James Joyce, will be of much interest to students and academic researchers.

I must mention that James is married to my cousin Patience (Sisi Abena Ansaa). Before he finally retired, James taught in universities in Ghana (Legon), Malawi, Nigeria, Belgium and the United Kingdom.

Here we go with what James Gibbs wrote to me: "I have read with interest the books you published and that my wife showed me. Congratulations on them. It has been particularly interesting to learn about people and places my wife has mentioned over the years. Over the years, I have written about Abiriw. For example, I wrote an obituary on (Jonas Kwasi) Yeboa Dankwa who was a wonderful correspondent and a great worker for the good of Abiriw. I also posted about the visit of Berners-Lee to the town."

THE DAY SIR TIM BERNERS-LEE, THE INVENTOR OF THE INTERNET, VISITED ABIRIW!

As narrated by James Gibbs.

Tim Berners-Lee in Ghana.

BBC Film Crew in Ghana.

Shared from a post originally written in September 2009.

Sir Timothy (born 8 June 1955), also known as TimBL, is an English computer scientist, best known as the inventor of the World Wide Web or the Internet.

"At about mid-day on the 20th September, 2009, I was walking along the main street of Abiriw, in the Eastern Region of Ghana when I saw a film-crew at work in the Communications Centre on the other side to the road.

On enquiry, I was told that a BBC team was filming for a series entitled 'Digital Revolution' (working title) that will be shown in the UK the following year.

It will examine the spread and the use of the Internet in Africa and will be partly built around Tim Berners-Lee, aka, it seems, as 'Timble'. Timble, who is rightly held in very high esteem for his work on the web, was inside the Communications Centre at Abiriw on the 20th September. He was talking to local users who were shown how to edit the Wikipedia entry for their town and how to set up blogs.

After leaving Abiriw, the crew went down to Adawso to film a farmer who talked about how he used the web to find out about new agricultural methods—notably drip irrigation schemes. I imagine that the series will raise questions about how new technology can help such farmers.

Mobile phones have certainly made an impact in rural Ghana, but the Internet is currently of limited value. The connection at the Abiriw Centre, to stick with that example, is always slow and sometimes 'down' altogether. Luckily, it was working quite well on the 20th.

It will be interesting to see how the Abiriw sequence comes across—if it survives the cutting room.

The 'fixer' who had brought them to Abiriw said: 'They almost didn't come because they were told Abiriw was 4 hours from Accra.' (It is in fact about 45 minutes from the 'Adenta Barrier'.)

Even after they had been to the place the team didn't have much sense of where they had been or how long it had taken them. One wrote of 'the town of Akropong/Abiriw' (sorry, that's two towns!) being 'three hours from Accra'. (Traffic in

Accra is often very bad so times are helpfully given from the edge of the built-up area.)

Another error that crept into postings by the production team was that internet access at the Communications Centre was free. It is not, though it is lower than the local commercial rate. It is also slower and more unreliable than the competition: Opre Ventures on the Akropong Bypass.

The internet link at Abiriw depends on the signal from the Apirede Resource Centre and that is lost if the equipment on the top of the tower of Calvary Presbyterian Church is out of position.

When it shifts, then the chap in charge of the Abiriw Centre has to climb to the top of the tower to adjust it. This is a scary climb as the staircase has no banisters. I wonder if Berners-Lee — or any member of the team made the ascent? I suspect not: Timble's time was short."

WHAT JAMES GIBBS WROTE ABOUT JONAS KWASI YEBOAH-DANKWA, A FOLKLORIC AND LITERARY LEGEND AND THE "CHIEF OKURASENI" OF ABIRIW

Before I share what James Gibbs wrote, let me take you back to part of what I wrote about this gentleman in my book, *Stories to Warm Your Heart*.

MFA WO NSA NKA NHWIREN! (KEEP YOUR HANDS OFF THE FLOWERS!)

I have heard it said that we are all captives of our childhood. I do not know how universally applicable this statement is, but I can say that I identify with it in many ways. Driving up and down the Akuapem hills never ceases to bring me a feeling of nostalgia. And even in more recent times, there are stories and memories to fall back on. One of the memories my children (now young adults) have is of a well-kept orchard and garden just across from our country home at Abiriw. They are part of a home belonging to the Yeboah-Dankwas. Walking past that house in the days when our children were young, we would all giggle as we saw a boldly written sign on the walls saying: "Mfa wo nsa nka nhwiren" meaning "keep your hands off the flowers."

The plants and the flowers and the fruit trees one could see always looked so beautiful and well kept.

The late Mr Jonas Yeboah-Dankwa, used to be a Bible translator, teacher and researcher among other things. He would always introduce himself to those he was meeting for the first time as *Okuraseni* which means Villager. He prided himself on being an *Okuraseni* who had become somebody, by the grace of God.

Now back to James Gibbs and what he wrote on Jonas Kwasi Yeboah-Dankwa.

"Jonas Kwasi Yeboa-Dankwa who died in May (2010) at the age of seventy-nine was a Ghanaian folklorist, teacher, and community activist with an international and national reputation. He exhausted himself in the service of his hometown, Abiriw-Akuapem in the Eastern Region.

Yeboa-Dankwa's international reputation rests on his work as a folklorist.

He studied at the University of Indiana during the early eighties and earned an MA with a thesis on Genres of Oral Literature and its Peculiarities in Africa in the Folktale of the Akan and Guan of Ghana (1984). His research papers on Akan and Guan folklore often survive only in mimeographed form, but there are exceptions. These include his contribution on *Storytelling of the Akan and Guan in Ghana,* in Richard K. Priebe's Ghanaian Literatures (1988), and *The Folktale of the Akan and the Guan of Ghana: The Audience and its Role* that appeared in Frankfurter Afrikanistische-Blatter (1992).

In Ghana, Yeboah-Dankwa will be remembered by many for his work as an educationist. He started teaching at Larteh Salem in 1952, and subsequent appointments included posts in the Junior Demonstration School at Akropong, in Jasikan Training College, the PTC Akropong, and, from 1979 to 1994, at the Language Centre, University of Ghana. It was at Legon that he found an academic 'home' —first as a Research Fellow and later as a Senior Research Fellow. There he influenced generations of students.

In retirement, Yeboah-Dankwa continued to teach. At that period, as earlier, his students included visiting academics embarking on periods of research or residence in Ghana and wanting to learn Twi.

Among his best-known publications are those related to teaching. These include the *Hwehwɛ Me Sua Me* series (1994) and *Basic Twi for Learners* (1998). These reflect his range and his educational formation.

Yeboah-Dankwa had received a sound Presbyterian training at the PTC, Akropong, and then went on to UST, Kumasi, the University College, Legon (where he finished a Diploma in Education in 1960), and the University College of Cape Coast (where he completed a bachelor's degree in Education in 1979). Yeboah-Dankwa's teaching was enlivened by his profound knowledge of Akan and Guan folklore, and by his own creative writing. He composed in both Twi and English, and his manuscripts include *Okere*

Guan Poems for Children (1985), and a collection of verses in English entitled *Some Daily Events of Man* (1988). He also made use of drama in his lessons and his play-scripts include *Mia w'ani, ɛbɛyɛ yie* (Agoru Bi) (drafted 1987, revised 2000 and 2001. English title: Struggle for Life: It will be well)."

PS. I was delighted to hear from a reader based in Delaware, the United States, that he had ordered a copy of Richard Priebe's book titled *Myth, Realism, and the West African Writer* after he read what I originally posted on Facebook. It is great to know that people are taking genuine interest in what we have been sharing.

"All those who met Yeboah-Dankwa soon heard about his passionate commitment to his hometown, Abiriw. Although his education and his need to earn a living took him away from the town—initially to Akropong, then further afield, his desire to contribute to what he called the 'social upliftment' of Abiriw was a dominant force in his life.

Many of the positive developments in Abiriw owe a huge debt to his vision, initiative, integrity, enthusiasm, organisational ability, and sacrificial self-giving. This is well illustrated by the establishment of the Abiriw Branch of the Ghana Library Board. In 1980, the dedication of Calvary Church (single-handedly built by the late Rexford Ayeh Darko of Mechanical Lloyd) released the old Presbyterian Church building for other purposes and Yeboah-Dankwa saw it could be used as a library. An activist working tirelessly on many levels, he pushed forward the Abiriw Library Project until, on 13 December 1991, the former chapel was opened as a branch of the Ghana Library Board. The formal opening took place in the presence of traditional office holders, local supporters, the South Korean Ambassador and the Director of the Ghana Library Board.

Another Abiriw project that benefited from Yeboah-Dankwa's willingness to devote his time, money and energy to positive initiatives is the Women's Centre. Officially opened by Dr Mary Grant on 4 October 1993, the Centre has been transformed into the Presbyterian Resource Centre. It currently offers a variety of vocational training and educational courses.

In the fullness of time, it may be possible to adequately chronicle Yeboah-Dankwa's contribution to the development of Abiriw, but, at this point, I would like simply to direct attention to his interest in the Abiriw Scholarship Fund, his efforts to rehabilitate local wells, his ideas on ecotourism and his role in establishing a teak nursery."

JAMES GIBBS ON JONAS KWASI YEBOAH-DANKWA

"Visitors to Abiriw can easily appreciate his intellectual and practical contribution to the community by visiting the Library. In that building, I would draw attention in particular to the collection of Abiriw-ana for which he donated copies of many of his publications and papers. The collection includes the talk he gave at the inauguration of a Branch of the Abiriw Union at Koforidua during 1991. It is entitled *The Great Pot Which Welcomes Strangers: The Emblem of Abiriw and its Interpretation. (Ɔsɛn kɛse a ɔgye ahɔho).* That paper, written in Twi and English, shows very clearly the way an internationally qualified folklorist can contribute to the self-awareness and self-knowledge of his community.

It is a feature of some traditions of obituary writing to conclude with a note about the nuclear family of the deceased. In this case, we can say that Kwasi Jonas Yeboah-Dankwa is survived by his wife, his five children (Akosua Adubea, Yaw Dankwa, Abena Adubea, Amma Dakoa, and Kwadwo Larbi) and by grandchildren. However, we should be aware that at the funeral of this great man, the streets of Abiriw will be thronged by many witnesses who will testify to the father-like qualities he showed to many. The witnesses will include those who have been helped, either individually or as a member of the community, by a remarkable folklorist, teacher and community activist.

May he rest in peace and the causes he supported go from strength to strength."

James Gibbs. Written on June 24, 2010.

WHEN THE MODERATOR CAME HOME
TO VICTORY, FAFRAHA

Sunday, December 18, 2016, was a great day in the annals of the Victory Congregation of the Presbyterian Church of Ghana, Fafraha near Adentan in Accra, the capital city of Ghana. The day also marked the 188th anniversary of the day when the first Basel missionaries landed in the Gold Coast (now Ghana). This makes the Presbyterian Church of Ghana the oldest, continuously existing church in Ghana.

It was a very joyous occasion as we welcomed the newly elected (and 17th) Moderator of the Presbyterian Church of Ghana to a thanksgiving service held in his honour.

The Moderator, Rt Rev. Professor Cephas Narh Omenyo, who until his elevation was the Provost of the College of Education of the University of Ghana, was the first Minister in charge of Victory and he spent almost 11 years there. In his own words, he spent slightly over a third of his 31 years of ministry at Victory. Moderator Omenyo called the attention of the church to the exemplary commitment of the early missionaries. These, he told us, were young professionals who left everything in order to serve the Lord in this part of the world. They had love and compassion, and their continued deaths from tropical diseases did not deter others from taking up their places. They died as martyrs and their blood had been the seed of the church. They were men and women of prayer and courage. They persevered and conquered because of their prayer life and fortitude. The Moderator asked the congregation never to forget the commitment and sacrifices of the missionaries. The Lord is looking for people who are ready to sacrifice and leave their comfort zones in order that the church will march on and reach out to those who need to hear the gospel. A rallying call to all of us, whether physically present at the service or not.

ONE OF THE HAPPIEST DAYS OF MY LIFE

OFORI PANIN SENIOR HIGH SCHOOL
55TH ANNIVERSARY SPEECH AND
PRIZE GIVING DAY
My Speech as GUEST SPEAKER
OPASS @ 55: THE ROLE OF STAKEHOLDERS

Mr Chairman, Members of the Board of Governors, Headmaster and staff, students, parents and guardians, old students ('Mpanyinfo'), members of the press, distinguished

Ladies and Gentlemen, I thank God Almighty for making me live to see this day. I cannot describe the feeling of joy welling up in me since I drove through the gates of this great school this morning with my wife Elioenai and my youngest daughter, Afua for today's function.

I remember a statement made by the late General Akwasi Amankwa Afrifa, then the Head of State of Ghana, when he spoke as Guest Speaker at Adisadel College, his old school. This was somewhere in the late 1960s. He told the gathering that his taking on that role was the greatest thing that had ever happened to him. This was a Head of State!

Mr Chairman, I feel the same way. I have been to Buckingham Palace for tea with Queen Elizabeth, her husband the Duke of Edinburgh and members of the British Royal Family in the exclusive Royal Tea Tent. That was in June 2010 and was facilitated by Professor Kwaku Danso-Boafo, the then High Commissioner of Ghana to the United Kingdom and a proud Opassian. Kwaku and I were classmates here at Opass. Thank you very much, Kwaku. I have written about the genesis of that visit in chapter one of my book *Stories to Warm Your Heart* under the heading 'From Abiriw to Buckingham Palace'. In December 2014, I was honoured as Guest of Honour at the 40th anniversary celebration of Dansoman Emmanuel Presbyterian Church, my mother church from where I moved to Victory Fafraha in 2009, an event broadcast live on Ghana Television. I have played other roles elsewhere but I want to confess that I feel extremely elated and highly honoured to have been invited to be the Guest Speaker at Ofori Panin, the school I am so proud of.

Thank you very much for this great honour.

If I had my way, I would sing along with Martin Rinkart his hymn:
Now thank we all our God
With hearts and hands and voices!
Who wondrous things hath done
In whom this world rejoices
Who from our mothers' arms
Has blessed us on our way
With countless gifts of love
And still is ours today.

Yes, I remember when I entered OPASS in September 1963, as a 12-year-old. I travelled with my mother from Abiriw, first to Koforidua, where she bought a box iron and a bucket for me. We then boarded an Anwona Patu, a small wooden commuter vehicle that used to ply the Koforidua/Tafo route. I carried three tins of sardines along with the very modest "provisions" my parents had been able to scrape together for me from their meagre resources. To this day I remember that a senior confiscated one tin of sardine; I made use of the second one and took the last tin back home to Abiriw to show my mother how I had been able to make a saving from what I took to school. As you can see, I started my financial planning a very long time ago.

Oh, thank God for His mercies. Let us count our blessings for how far the Lord has brought us. I thank God for the dedication of the pioneer staff we had here at OPASS. The sense of discipline, direction and sense of purpose of Mr S. T. Ampofo, the Addo Fenings, V. B. Freemans, Gabriel Etus, Twum Dansos, W. E. Amoahs and Boniface Adjeis of my days are legendary. I also know that the G. A. Gyimahs and

Kwame Amo Dakos and the subsequent and current crop of leadership at the school have carried and are carrying the torch handed over to them well.

Mr Chairman, I am very mindful of the theme for this great occasion, which is OPASS @ 55: THE ROLE OF STAKEHOLDERS.

I would categorise our major Stakeholders as the students, teachers and other staff members, parents and the products of the school, namely old students.

The message I have is a composite one directed at each group. But I want you the students to take particular note of the points I am going to raise. I have twelve points in all which I am calling Agenda 212.

AGENDA 212

1. Remember why you are here. You are here to study and to be guided to become useful citizens in future. Never forget why you are here. There is a time for everything under the sun. You are not here to marry or to engage in relationships. The time for that will come. Remember why you are here.

2. Be disciplined in everything you do, whether it is going to the dining hall, to the classroom, to the sports field or to take part in other school activities like worship services or cleaning. The disciplined person does what needs to be done, whether he or she feels like it or not. It is like exercise or dieting. It is day after day after day, rain or shine. Discipline is the key to personal greatness.

3. Understand that success is the sum of small efforts, repeated day in and day out. The farmer understands this better than most of us. The farmer knows what he wants

and is patient. The cocoa farmer in particular has to wait for a number of years before harvest starts. While waiting, the farmer keeps tending and watering. Be patient.

4. Success is not overnight. It is the progressive realisation of a predetermined goal. Be faithful and consistent in the little things. I want every young person in Ghana to hear this and to let it sink in. Be faithful in the little things.

5. Cultivate the reading habit. Reading will give you uncommon understanding. You will learn from the experiences of others. I am a living testimony of the benefits of reading. I devoured book upon book, other than my school textbooks and I have continued to do so till now. Become a reader.

6. Additionally, be careful of the friends you make and keep. Keep the friends who will make you a better person rather than lead you into trouble. Choose good friends.

7. The books you read, the friends you keep and the food you eat will determine in no small way the type of person you will become in future. I am pleased that the friends I made at OPASS have increased me, rather than diminish me. That is because they were, and have remained such good friends. Friends like Ambassadors Kwasi Baah-Boakye and Kwaku Danso-Boafo, Justices Aduama Osei and Julius Ansah, Dr Nicholas Smart-Yeboah, Dr S. T. Djaba (TT), Major Fred Twum Acheampong (retd), Nana Architect Ameyaw (Abomosuhene), Kwaku Osseo-Asare, Dr Kwame Ampofo Koranteng, the late Sampson Amoako Nuamah and many, many others.

8. Do not live aimlessly. Set yourself a goal and work towards it. Have your eye on something bigger than what

you are now. Hold on to some dream, some hope, some overarching something to sustain you and propel you to become what you want to be in the future. No vision and you perish!

9. Do not limit yourself and do not allow others to diminish you. Let no one despise your youth, as the Apostle Paul advised his young friend Timothy.

10. To our beloved country Ghana, I want us to remember that we owe it to ourselves as a nation to make our knowledge work, to put our training and education to good use. If we have all the training and education in the world, and yet fail to apply them towards making our lives, and those of others better, then we are to be pitied. Let us demonstrate, by words and deeds, as individuals and as a nation that we have through the investments made in us by our parents and institutions, imbibed the life skills to improve on our destinies.

11. Preparation. Preparation. Preparation. Everything I have said can be summed up in being a people who are prepared to face the challenges of life and leave a legacy for the next generation. "Quality is never an accident. It is always the result of intelligent effort," so said John Ruskin. Therefore make use of the opportunities around you. Create the future you want by making use of the opportunities at OPASS. Some of us did so, and by the grace of God we are what we are today.

12. I end with an example taken from my book, *Pearls of Wisdom*, published by Step Publishers in June 2016. "The Germans did not win the 2014 edition of the World Cup by accident. They had a 10-year plan which they pursued meticulously. It is also noteworthy that they built a state-

of-the-art training ground costing millions of dollars in a remote fishing village near their base in Brazil, where they were able to train comfortably and consolidate on their team spirit."

Mr Chairman, members of the Board of Governors, staff and students of OPASS, parents and guardians, old students ('Mpanyinfo'), distinguished Ladies and Gentlemen, I hope that I have been able to inspire you to look forward with hope about the kind of future you want to see yourself inhabiting.

I want you to know, one more time, that I am eternally grateful to you all for honouring me with this role. It is William Arthur Ward who said that feeling gratitude and not expressing it is like wrapping a present and not giving it. As a token of my gratitude and as a past Library Prefect, I am pleased to present to the school library a total of 60 copies of my books comprising 20 of each title, namely, *Pearls of Wisdom*, *Stories to Warm Your Heart* and *Nuggets for Victorious Living*.

It is also my singular pleasure to present to the school, through the Board Chairman, a cheque for GH¢10,000 from BEIGE Capital for the acquisition of books for the school library.

Hail to thee our Great OPASS

Alma mater.

Indeed, your sons and daughters sing your praises. God bless Ofori Panin Senior High School and may OPASS grow from strength to strength. God bless our homeland Ghana.

Thank you.

7

ESTHER AFUA OCLOO OF NKULENU INDUSTRIES

A BUSH GIRL COMES TO TOWN

On April 18, 2017, Google honoured Esther Afua Ocloo with their Doodle for the day. This was a significant recognition of one of the greatest people Ghana has produced, Esther Afua Ocloo (born Esther Afua Nkulenu).

A Google Doodle is a special, temporary alteration of the logo on Google's homepage that is intended to celebrate holidays, events, achievements and people.

BUT WHO WAS ESTHER AFUA OCLOO?

With the encouragement of my brother and friend R. B. Perbi and in consultation with her family, I am going to take you on a narrative of the life, times and achievements of this remarkable woman whose influence lives on. She died on

February 8, 2002. She would have been 98 years old on April 18, the day Google honoured her.

The Early Years

On Saturday, March 23, 2002, Ghana held a state funeral at the State House, Accra, for Mrs Esther Afua Ocloo (born Esther Afua Nkulenu). President John Agyekum Kufuor, Vice President Aliu Mahama and many dignitaries were present to bid farewell to a famous daughter of the land. President Kufuor delivered an eulogy to her.

Who was Esther Afua Ocloo of Nkulenu Industries fame?

Esther Afua Ocloo was born at Peki on April 18, 1919. She came from a poor background, but took her basic education seriously. Through her diligent studies she won a Cadbury scholarship to attend Achimota School in 1936. Esther entered Achimota, the most prestigious and best-endowed educational institution in the then Gold Coast as a village girl (I would prefer to use my favourite term *Okuraseni*).

The environment was completely new and strange to her. Esther could barely cope with the modernity she encountered at Achimota. One of her challenges with modernity at Achimota, was using gadgets in Home Science classes. She nearly gave up but for the encouragement she received from her teacher, Miss Janet Asare. Her encouragement contributed to Esther's success. The lessons learned made it possible for her to produce her first batch of jam, marmalade and orange squash.

Another challenge was with the English language. She was the butt of jokes as she struggled to polish her spoken English. Her classmates recall her peculiar ways of pronouncing some words, often evoking peals of laughter and a lot of teasing in the classroom and in the dormitory. Nothing would however deter this determined *Okuraseni*. She would continue whatever she was saying to the end. She graduated from Achimota in 1940. Happily, she could speak "Achimota English" by then.

Hard Times and a Silver Lining

Soon after leaving Achimota in 1940, Esther found herself jobless and stranded in Accra. She fell on hard times. There was no help in sight to help her move on. She survived only by the benevolence of some relatives from Peki who lived in Accra. But God moves in mysterious ways, His wonders to perform. An aunt by name Mrs Josephine Mensah (née Nkulenu), who had earlier postponed her own marriage on two occasions in order to support Esther while the latter was in school, visited Accra. This aunt was so deeply moved by her niece's difficult living conditions that she gave Esther ten shillings as pocket money to help make ends meet.

Esther, who had learned how to prepare marmalade in her Home Science classes at Achimota, took a bold decision. Instead of spending all the money on consumption, she invested 6 shillings into buying inputs (oranges, sugar, firewood, jars) for producing marmalade. She produced 12 jars of marmalade which she hawked around Government offices in Accra the next day.

By 10 am that morning, she had sold all the marmalade and realised 12 shillings. The *Okuraseni* felt like a millionaire. A fire lit in her mind. She knew what she wanted to do.

The Decision to Go into Business

Esther decided to go into business. She put up what was an apology of a factory with planks and roofing sheets she bought from the scrap market at Kokompe in Accra and went straight into business producing marmalade and orange squash. Within six months she had attracted attention from Achimota School, the Royal West African Frontier Force (which was based on the western compound of Achimota) and others. She became a regular supplier of marmalade and orange squash to these.

Esther Afua Ocloo had her eyes on the future. She could think far! She was frugal in the handling of the proceeds from her fledgling "cottage industry". She saved everything she could and decided to travel abroad to study food processing. By now she had established a reputation for industry and therefore won additional financial support from Achimota, the Colonial Office and a few friends which enabled her to travel to the United Kingdom.

Further Studies and Beyond

She studied at the Good Housekeeping School of Cookery in London, Bristol University and at Pitman's College (for business management). She returned home in 1952 and in addition to scaling up her operation to Nkulenu Food Industry, set up the Modern Caterers Company with her friend, the late Mrs Carlis-Paitoo. She used this as a vehicle to cater for various banquets and private parties in the Gold Coast. She also ran a mobile canteen, known as "meals on wheels".

By the early 1960s, when I first heard the name and her Nkulenu products as a student, she had become the main manufacturer and supplier of canned Ghanaian foods such as groundnut soup, jollof rice, beans in *dzomi* and palaver sauce to the Ghana Armed Forces. As for her marmalade and orange juice, they were by then national staples at breakfast tables.

It is significant to note that Esther was the first to introduce convenience to Ghanaian cooking by developing the palm nut soup base. Up till now, products like the palm nut soup base, palm wine and kenkey are much sought after by Ghanaians in the diaspora. Enter any African shop in New York, London or any major city in the West with a sizeable Ghanaian population and you will be sure to find Nkulenu products.

Marriage

In 1959, she got married to Stephen Kobla Ocloo, who became her adviser and business partner. According to Mr Ocloo, who is still alive, they first met in June 1958 at a meeting of representatives and owners of small businesses in Ghana called and chaired by Esther.

The purpose of the meeting was to prepare a memorandum towards the work of a Committee the Government wanted to look into the needs of indigenous industries. The then Esther Afua Nkulenu asked for a volunteer to assist in the preparation of the memorandum. Her appeal drew a blank until he, Stephen, stepped in to help. That was the beginning of a relationship which culminated in marriage one year later.

Esther was not only interested in developing her own business. She had a desire to see local businesses develop and produce goods for local consumption. To help overcome

117

the prejudice against locally produced goods, she helped form the Federation of Ghanaian Industries to cater for the interests of Ghanaian manufacturers in 1958.

Esther was elected the first President of the Association (now the Association of Ghana Industries). She served in that capacity until 1961. In 1973, she was again elected President and served a two-year term. In 1978 the Association again elected her to the Presidency.

Her Achievements

Esther was passionate about the empowerment of women. She did not forget the hardships she had gone through in her early life and felt that she owed a duty to herself and society to help women (and the youth) to develop self-employable skills. To this end, she immersed herself in a number of projects including the following:

- Establishing a vocational school in the fifties to train unemployed girls in self-employable skills.
- Turning the Peki Clinic into a full hospital through the efforts of Peki women, under her leadership.
- Upgrading the economic status of women at Peki through their acquisition of self-employable skills, including the making of tie-dye and batik clothing. She also taught them how to make beads and dolls.
- Setting up a farm for the youth at Agomenya for the cultivation of food crops and animal husbandry (piggery and poultry). She also taught how to cultivate mushroom and breed snails.
- Establishing the African Women Entrepreneurial Training Centre at Peki to train young girls and upgrade the skills of women entrepreneurs in

Food Processing, Textiles (broad loom weaving), Dressmaking, and basics of Business Management.
- Assisting the National Council on Women and Development in establishing income generating projects across the country.

Additionally, she founded a number of Non-Governmental Organisations (NGOs), including:
- Ghana Federation of Business and Professional Women.
- Aid to Artisans Ghana.
- The Sustainable End of Hunger Foundation (with the prize money from her 1990 Africa Leadership Prize for Sustainable End of Hunger).

Esther embarked on a programme to share her knowledge with women who cook and sell products on the streets, a common phenomenon in Ghana. She found that a woman selling rice and stew on the side of the street was making more money than most women in office jobs. That was a revelation which spurred her on in her mission.

She promoted the availability of credit to women with small loans along the lines of the Grameen Bank pioneered by Mohammed Yunus in Bangladesh. This was to help them to establish and run their own businesses. This passion led her to become a founding member and the first Chairman of the Board of Directors of Women's World Banking.

Her Political Orientation

Esther was firm in her belief that political office and power should be used for social engineering and development. She therefore did not shy away from active involvement in politics.

In 1969 she stood for elections on the ticket of the Progress Party, led by Dr K. A. Busia, in the South Dayi constituency in the Volta Region. The Progress Party won the national elections but Esther lost her bid for a Parliamentary seat.

She had been identified in the political space in the country! On January 13, 1972, there was a military coup led by the then Col. I. K. Acheampong and the Busia government was overthrown. The soldiers came for Esther and her husband. Her husband was released not long afterwards but Esther was sent to the James Town prison and incarcerated for a period of three months. For what? To date no one has been able to tell what her offence was. In any event she was not even tried by a court. Those were the days of jungle justice. Thanks be to God for how far He has brought us through the courage of those who believed in the rule of law.

Her arrest and imprisonment sent shock waves through the business community. Many in the community, and family and friends, tried all they could to get her released but their efforts came to no avail.

Prison did not break her spirit, however. Nor did her resolve to make things better wherever she found herself. She took it on herself to disinfect the cells. She taught the other female inmates needlework. Esther led morning devotions and Sunday morning services. It is reported that the prison authorities could not hide their amazement at the zeal with which she went about these activities.

Esther Ocloo wanted to see many women in politics. This desire led her to establish the Ghanaian Women Initiative

Foundation (GAWIF) after her release from prison. The objective of GAWIF was to encourage and support women to stand for elections irrespective of their political party affiliation. She sought the support of women in the media and sponsored programmes on radio to encourage people to vote for female candidates.

Her Faith Life

Esther Afua Ocloo took her faith in God seriously. Her credo was that, "Those who trust in the Lord shall renew their strength. They will soar on wings like eagles, they will run and not grow weary, they will walk and not faint" (Isa 40:31).

She spent the early part of the day having devotions in a prayer room she put up as an extension to the family residence at Madina in Accra.

She was a firm believer in the 3 T's: Tithe, Talent and Time. "Give out freely and you will end up being rewarded in places you have not even sown," she was fond of saying. She believed in putting God first in everything. It is reported that she led a selfless life, sharing her time, money and talent with countless people.

To this end, she helped to establish the Evangelical Presbyterian Church at Madina in addition to other congregations in the West Volta Presbytery. She was instrumental in the formation of the women's group of the church known as "Bible Class", whose objective is to study the Bible and to promote Christian living and home management.

Her lifestyle and dressing habits exemplified her deep-seated Christian commitment.

Her Awards

Esther Afua Ocloo's efforts won her many honours, both in and outside Ghana.

In 1969, she was decorated by the Government of Ghana with the Grand Medal.

In 1977, a Doctor of Science (Honoris Causa) was conferred on her by the Kwame Nkrumah University of Science and Technology.

In 1990, she and Nigerian President Gen. Olusegun Obasanjo were co-recipients of the African Leadership Prize for Sustainable End of Hunger. Esther became the first woman to receive the African Leadership Prize for Sustainable End of Hunger. The award ceremony was held in New York and was graced by luminaries like Robert McNamara, US Defence Secretary under President John F. Kennedy, Andrew Young, Jesse Jackson, Michaela Walsh (President of Women's World Banking) and Diana Ross.

In 1993, she won the Laureate of Gottlieb Dutweiller Prize in Switzerland for training African women and for philanthropy.

In 1998, she was honoured by Beijing Women of Rochester, New York, USA, as one of 100 Heroines for the cause of Women in the 20th century.

In 2001, she won the African Women Entrepreneurial Excellence Award, Kenya.

LESSONS FROM HER LIFE
Lesson Number 1: Do Not Despise Small Beginnings

I want our young people in particular to hear this loud and clear. Every big business you see (and most certainly admire) started small. You have to listen to the stories of successful people to learn about the daunting obstacles and lack they faced when they started their undertakings.

What marked them out is that they had a dream. They had a vision of what they wanted to do, and they kept that dream and vision in view. All the time. Day after day after day. They did not look back, and no discouragement would make them abandon their plans.

Through diligence, persistence and focus, Esther Afua Ocloo was able to build a thriving business whose beginnings were the seed of ten shillings.

It is like being given GH¢100 today by a well-wisher. I can imagine someone asking what he or she is going to do with that amount of money in the face of all the needs facing them in present-day Ghana or even elsewhere. Yet, that GH¢100 faithfully used, can produce fast-moving products needed by the average consumer to land a profit which can be reinvested. Go and speak to any of the big names who run their own businesses to check out the veracity or otherwise of what is being stated here.

The word for you is, do not sit down waiting for that big sum of money. Put the little you have to work. Look round you. Your eyes will be opened to seemingly little needs of people as they rush to work or move about. You can turn that little seed into something that will meet a need. And you will gradually build that something into something better and bigger incrementally.

Do not despise small beginnings.

Lesson Number 2: Bring Hope to Others

We do not live for ourselves. How I wish this would sink in deeply in each of us. If it did, the nonsense we see going on around us with *galamsey*, to cite only one obvious example, would not be tolerated in our country. Apart from living to please God, we owe it to ourselves to influence lives. This is especially so when God has by His grace blessed and elevated us. I am of the view that the satisfaction you get from life stems from what you have done, or will do, to bring hope, relief, joy and some form of assistance to other people. In a very real sense, we were made to give and to serve. I believe that it is because that man whose barns were filled to the brim and overflowing forgot this that the Lord Jesus Christ described him as a rich fool, and his life was taken from him. All his bragging about the expansion he was going to carry out to accommodate the bumper harvest came to nought. (The "Parable of the Rich Fool" in Lk 12:13-21 in the Bible.)

Esther Afua Nkulenu brought hope to others. She did this through the numerous schemes she established to give self-employable skills to the youth and women in particular. These initiatives lifted many out of poverty and gave them a sense of self-worth they would never have had otherwise.

Let us make it our aim to bring hope to others. Nothing is too small. Just have the right frame of mind and go ahead and help someone.

Lift up someone. Bring hope to others.

Lesson Number 3: Money Amplifies Character

In a sense, every spending decision is a spiritual decision. That is why it is easy to tell what anyone's priorities are just by looking at their cheque books or at how they spend their money.

Your values will be evident from how and on what you spend your money.

Esther established the Sustainable End of Hunger Foundation with the prize money from her 1990 Africa Leadership Prize for Sustainable End of Hunger. The foundation acquired 62 acres of farmland to establish the Agomanya Youth Settlement Farm Project and also the African Women Entrepreneurial Training Centre in the Volta Region. This laudable initiative was borne out of her desire to help women and young people engaging in productive agricultural and other projects that would improve their economic status. It would have been perfectly legitimate for her to spend the huge prize money on herself and her family. She had earned it.

But she had a wider vision and understanding of money. She saw it as a tool to leave a legacy of hope and as a means to leave the world a better place than she met it through lifting the vulnerable out of helplessness and hopelessness.

By the way, this message applies to all, whether you "have money" (crude translation from the vernacular) or you consider yourself a "have not." The harsh reality is that often those who consider themselves as "have nots" are the ones who are most covetous of money. They spend their time fantasising about money and may even be prepared to use unorthodox and illegal means to get their "share."

Yes, money amplifies character.

"Do not lay up for yourselves treasures on earth, where moth and rust destroy and where thieves break in and steal; but lay up for yourselves treasures in heaven, where neither moth nor rust destroys and where thieves do not break in and steal. For where your treasure is, there your heart will be also" (Matt 6:19-21 NKJV).

Lesson Number 4: Appreciate the Value of Agriculture in Nation Building

Esther knew the role agriculture could play in national development and growth. She was like her kinsman, Owura Amu, who never stopped asking that agriculture be given pride of place in our educational system. Incidentally both of them hailed from Peki. The people of Peki must be proud to have produced, and indeed continue to produce, such great people.

Listen to Esther Afua Ocloo:

"Our problem here in Ghana is that we have turned our back on agriculture. Over the past 40 years, since the beginning of compulsory education, we have been mimicking the West. We are now producing youth with degrees who don't want to work in the fields or have anything to do with agriculture."

Let us give all the support required to agriculture so that Ghana will be self-sufficient in food production. By so doing we shall also be providing jobs to our people.

FINALLY

At her state funeral in Accra, Rev. Dr Boamah of the E. P. Church delivered an inspiring sermon entitled, "A Bush Girl Goes to Town". He drew lessons from Esther's life struggles, faith in God and accomplishments to inspire others.

President John Agyekum Kufuor also at her state funeral declared: "She was a creator and we need many people of her calibre to build our nation.

126

"She was a real pillar . . . worthy of emulation in our efforts to build our nation. Her good works in the promotion of development in Ghana cannot be measured".

Meet Stephen Kobla Ocloo, husband of Esther Afua Ocloo of Nkulenu Industries

I made my way to the Madina residence of the 88-year-old Mr Ocloo one Sunday afternoon. After doing my series on the legendary Esther Afua Ocloo, I was eager to meet her husband, who I heard was alive.

Setting up the appointment involved linking up with his daughter Vincentia in California and his son Kwaku in Accra. My perseverance paid off. It was a pleasure to meet Mr Ocloo. He was behind his desktop computer. He was reviewing a strategy document dealing with the future direction of Nkulenu Industries. He told me that the vision of the founder, his late wife, was to preserve and process all Ghanaian dishes and beverages and make them convenient foods. That vision is as relevant as when it was first espoused by Esther Afua Ocloo in the mid-1950s.

Mr Ocloo told me that kenkey, palm wine (bottled) and palm nut base are the company's most popular export products. These are available in Europe, the Americas and the Far East. He showed me a bottle of palm wine which he was proud to say was still fresh after 5 years. This is one example of a locally grown industry which has braved the odds and continues to contribute its quota to our needs. This is what entrepreneurship is all about, that is, to identify a need and provide a solution to it.

Mr Stephen Kobla Ocloo, by all indications, is an active person for his age. He is also head of the wider Ocloo family spreading from Accra, Keta to Togo, Benin and Gabon.

Why Gabon, I asked? To which he explained that one of his uncles went to live in Gabon, married there and died there. The family in Ghana has kept very strong links and the descendants of his uncle have on occasion in the past travelled to Ghana to stay with his family in order to learn English.

8

HER LEGACY LIVES ON: REMEMBERING A MATRIARCH
YAA OKYEREBEA ADU LABI

Some people live their lives in simple, unassuming ways and yet end up influencing others in ways that are far reaching. Their influence is borne out of a deep abiding sense of charity, which in turn is as a result of their never forgetting their humble beginnings. One such person whose influence is so much in evidence many years after her death, is my own mother. Her life epitomises the following statement:

> "It is in giving that we receive, and it is through dying that we are born to eternal life." — St. Francis of Assisi

Mrs Yaa Adu Labi was born at Kokofa near Suhum on Thursday, October 2, 1919 to Ben Opare Addo and Adelaide Akua Oye, both of blessed memory. Like most Akuapems of those times, her parents had an "Akuraa" or hamlet/cottage, for want of a better description, where they retreated regularly to tend to their farms.

She started school rather later than normal because her father did not think it was necessary for girls to go to school. Girls were meant to help at home, on the farm and to run chores till they got married. This was the belief of many fathers in those days.

One day, some Basel missionaries walked over from next door Akropong to persuade members of the Church at Abiriw that they should send both their daughters and sons to school. This was a campaign they had started at Akropong and nearby towns including Larteh and Mamfe. Her father listened carefully and agreed to send her to school. She must have been about 9 years old.

However, she had a remarkable start. Instead of proceeding to class two after class one, she was "jumped" (promoted) straight to class four. She was simply brilliant!

From Abiriw Presbyterian Primary School, "Auntie", as she was affectionately called by her children as well as her numerous nephews, nieces, and relations proceeded to the Basel Mission Girls School, Agogo.

She was at Agogo Girls School from 1933 to 1936. She then entered the Basel (Presbyterian) Training College, Agogo in January 1937 and graduated as a teacher in December 1939.

Auntie's seven years at Agogo were most enjoyable. It was at Agogo that many of the life skills that came in so handy in her adult years were acquired. She became an all-rounder, who knitted, embroidered, sewed, baked and cooked. I remember how she sewed clothes (including what was then called "twakoto" for me) and knitted sweaters and pullovers for us. She had a special method for baking cakes using a coal pot. Those cakes were truly delicious!

The teachers who impacted her life included Awuraa Ackerman, Awuraa Goetz, Awuraa Schlatter, Awuraa Mischler, Miss Kwabi, Miss Amartey and Miss Asare. Incidentally, Frau (Awuraa) Friedel Mischler later became my godmother and we had a very happy relationship during my childhood.

Auntie used to regale us her children and numerous friends and relations with stories about her Agogo days. The attempts by the Basel missionaries to speak to the school girls in Twi were particularly tickling.

One particular missionary was said to precede every sentence in Twi with *"Ti sɛ yi na"*. So an admonition to the girls would go like this. *"Ti sɛ yi na mmɔfra mo yɛ mmɔfra bɔne"*, meaning "you girls are being naughty."

The Second World War broke out when Auntie was in her final year at College. Germans were declared enemies. That was to be expected. Rather unexpectedly, the serene atmosphere at Agogo was interrupted when British troops came to the town to take captive Germans there. There were a number working at the hospital. Awuraa Schlatter (a Swiss German married to a German) was detained alongside other German enemies by the British Colonial authorities because they assumed she was German. She was not. She was Swiss, but like all the other missionaries, from the German speaking area of Switzerland. Confusion and panic gripped the compound. The "enemies" were put in a truck by armed soldiers. The school girls were distraught and lined up to comfort their detained teachers and other captives.

The girls were wailing. The other teachers lifted their voices in unison. At this juncture Awuraa Schlatter burst out weeping and said: *"Ti sɛ yi na mmɔfra anka menyɛ German ni oo, na Owura nti, Owura nti, Owura nti!"*

This may be interpreted as "Girls, please note that I am not really German. I have been taken captive all because of my husband who is German. It is all because of my husband! All because of my husband."

Fortunately, the captives were released after a short period of detention in Kumasi when the British colonial administration realised that they were innocent missionaries.

THE TEACHER WHO HAD NO SHOES

On qualifying as a teacher, Auntie was posted to the Sunyani Government School where she taught domestic science from 1940 to 1944.

It is interesting to note that prior to her qualifying as a teacher, she had never worn shoes.

Anytime she pleaded with her father for a pair of shoes, her father insisted on his "no shoes" policy for his children. How times have changed! He always offered her a choice between shoes and school. Of course she knew better and always opted for education.

However things took a different turn when her father bought her first pair of shoes on her becoming a teacher. The reason for his change of heart? Father had never seen a barefooted teacher and he did not want his teacher daughter to set a record by being the first! Do not get too excited though, because those shoes were bought on credit. She paid for them from her first salary.

Those were very precious shoes nevertheless.

It is reported that Auntie excelled as a teacher at Sunyani. She also made lifelong friends who remained in contact till the time of her death.

We came to know some of these, including the children of Master Oppong, one of them being Mr Yaw Oppong, former Chairman of Scripture Union Ghana and a retired Director of Engineering of the Electricity Company of Ghana.

Based on her good performance at Sunyani, Auntie was selected to do a one-year specialist home science course at Achimota College (January–December 1945). Among her mates was the late Florence Koranteng, our kinswoman from Abiriw. Achimota was a wonderful experience for her. Among the lifelong friends she made there was the legendary Kofi Antobam, the carver of the Presidential stool of Ghana, who was on the staff there.

After Achimota, she taught at Anumle Government School from where she was posted to Kibi Government School. After Kibi came Oda, Akwatia, Abiriw, Osenase, Kumasi and Asante Asokore. By this time she was married and she went to most of these places with Papa, a Headteacher who later became Abiriwhene (Chief of Abiriw).

She was transferred to Larteh from Asokore before being posted to Akuapem Mampong Girls School in 1963 where she was promoted Headmistress in 1965. After a highly successful stay at Mampong Girls School she was posted to Akwatia in 1969 as Headmistress of the Akwatia Presbyterian Middle School where she retired in 1974.

Mrs Yaa Adu Labi left an enduring legacy and touched so many lives. She was generous to a fault. She was compassionate and showed concern for the well-being of orphans and the destitute. During her old age she resorted to directing the poor and needy she could no longer help to us her children.

In spite of our objections to her style, each of us has in one way or the other inherited this trait of hers. We are the better for it.

She was a firm believer in the value of education and left no stone unturned to ensure that her children as well as siblings and numerous relations who lived in her household took their education seriously.

A VORACIOUS READER

Her husband, Nana Otutu Bagyire IV, Abiriwhene, who predeceased her in 1979, was also a firm believer in education, being himself a renowned historian and Fellow of the Historical Society of Ghana. This explains why reading was such a pastime in all the young people who passed through her hands.

Auntie was a voracious reader. As a rule she finished any book (however voluminous) she laid hands on within 48 hours. She kept reading till about three years to her death when her eyes became weakened. Even then she used to listen to audio recordings of books. Her granddaughter Akofa Bentsi-Enchill made sure that she had a regular supply of audio books. She could not live without books.

Her love of reading had a positive effect on her children. Though poor, we grew up in a home where books were never in short supply. I remember *The Basket of Flowers*

(*Das Blumenkörbchen*) by Christoph von Schmid, a Catholic priest, a deeply moving book about a gross injustice done an innocent man. He ended up in prison for many long years. Eventually the truth came out and he was exonerated. The lesson in the book was how this man who had suffered grave injustice and had been imprisoned for years and had gone grey-headed readily forgave those who had wronged him.

I also remember *A Town Like Alice* set in Alice Springs in the Australian outback and other books which allowed me to travel in my mind's eyes to far-off places. I must say that one of my unfulfilled dreams is to travel to Australia to visit Adelaide, Canberra, Alice Springs and the Gold Coast, all as a result of books I read at home due to my mother's influence. (There are two other unfulfilled dreams of mine but this is not the time to write about them, though they are rather mundane and closer to home.)

I have a confession to make, however. I now no longer relish the desire to travel to Australia as much as I did when I was young. The simple reason is that I cannot imagine being in the air across the never-ending sea continuously for the 16 or so hours travellers take to get there. I have so far resisted all the gentle attempts of the children of my brother-in-law, Apostle Ato Addison (former General Secretary of The Church of Pentecost), to get me to visit them in Australia. They live in Australia with their families and grew up with my children in Ghana.

Auntie encouraged us to read any book we could lay our hands on. Fiction, history, biographies, autobiographies and current affairs. When we became adults and set up our homes, we had to ensure that there was always something for her to read when she came visiting. If not, she would invariably blurt out, "So is there nothing to read in this house?"

HER FAITH LIFE

Auntie was a family person who loved not only her children but all her numerous relations. This is no exaggeration. Her home was regularly frequented by well-wishers from far and near.

She was in turn loved and cherished in a special way.

On retirement she lived at Abiriw with her husband. For a period after the death of the late Abiriwhene (her husband), she spent some time with her daughter Amma at Okuapemman School. She later joined her eldest daughter Akua at Tesano, Accra, to help with the care of Akua's children. Of course, she always returned to Abiriw regularly to see to her numerous family obligations.

While at Tesano, she fellowshipped with the North Kaneshie Presbyterian Church. She became an instant celebrity with the Women's Fellowship due to her encyclopaedic knowledge of the Bible and the old Twi hymn book. It is said that any time there was a Bible quiz competition, there would be an outburst of joy when she appeared, because her group was sure to win. On occasions when she was away at Abiriw, emissaries would be sent to fetch her to Tesano any time a quiz competition was going to take place.

She knew each hymn and each verse of the old Twi hymn book, from cover to cover. But even more importantly, she was a Christian who was sure of her salvation.

She took her relationship with her Lord and Saviour Jesus Christ very seriously and made sure that she kept her integrity with her God. She lived by the biblical injunction in Romans 12:18 that "if possible, so far as it depends on you, live peaceably with all." She was a woman of peace.

On her 80th birthday, October 2, 1999, her children organised a grand birthday celebration in her honour. It was a real celebration of life especially as the festivities took place at her then brand new residence, Okyerebea Lodge, built to celebrate her while alive rather than "memorialise" her after her death.

It was a joy to see her children, grandchildren, in-laws, relations and old girls from Agogo feasting, singing and dancing in gratitude to God for the great things He had done in the life of Auntie.

THE FINAL LAP

For about 10 years before her call to glory, Auntie lived a serene life at Abiriw with periodic trips to Accra for medical check-ups.

Like every indigene of the Akuapem ridge, she loved her hometown. A song she loved and taught others to sing about her hometown was:

Baabi nni hɔ a ɛyɛ fɛ
Sen yɛn ankasa yɛn kurom
Ehɔ na yɛbɛboa yɛn ho ano
Wɔ nyɛdua ase.

In short, the song is saying that there is nowhere as enjoyable as one's hometown. It is there that we sit under the shade tree and have fun.

She was healthy for her age and had a very sharp mind. She remembered the birthdays of her grandchildren. She also remembered the exact date on which she stopped eating corned beef. Now, all you lovers of corned beef, prepare for the next sentence. She stopped eating corned beef when someone she knew opened a tin and found a wedding ring in the can. This confirmed a suspicion she had harboured for some time that corned beef contained human flesh and bones!

On Saturday, June 2, she was lively and received a number of visitors. She was taken ill suddenly on Sunday, June 3 and was rushed to the Tetteh Quarshie Memorial Hospital where she passed away peacefully in the night.

There was a very interesting twist of events that Sunday morning. I was at Okyerebea Lodge that morning because I was the preacher at Abiriw Calvary Presbyterian Church that day. I had gone there the previous day with my daughter Eunice Adotey (Awurabena). Before leaving the house, I passed through her wing to let her know I was on my way to church. She was sitting on the couch in her sitting room, looking unusually quiet. She nodded her head and I left.

Just as the preparatory hymn before the start of my sermon was called, an Usher walked over to tell me that someone was looking for me. I felt irritated, and wondered aloud why anyone would want to see me at a time like this. I ignored the call. Then a second message came, this time with the news that my mother had collapsed and her caretaker had called for help and got our next-door neighbour to rush her to the Tetteh Quarshie Hospital at Mampong Akuapem.

I had to think quickly. I did not want to cause consternation in the chapel, knowing how closely-knit the congregation was. I turned to the then District Minister, Rev. Kwaku Opare Darko (I call him Kwaku). I told him, "Kwaku, I am told that Auntie has been rushed to the hospital. Can you please follow up on her and I shall be there as soon as I am done with my sermon?" Rev. Opare Darko got up and left without a word to anyone, and I followed up as soon as I got down from the pulpit, again without a word to anyone, apart from beckoning to my daughter to get up and follow me.

On getting to the hospital, the physician on duty informed me that my mother had suffered a stroke and that they were trying to stabilise her. I went over to the ward immediately and was relieved to note that she was conscious and had most of her sensory powers working. She appeared to be in pain and was uncomfortable.

During her few hours stay at the hospital, many loved ones (including all her children in Ghana, the only exception being Sister Akua who was based in The Hague as a Judge of the International Criminal Court) visited her and were able to exchange pleasantries with her.

Auntie passed away that night, after we had left the hospital. The Medical Superintendent of the hospital, Dr Augustine Sarfo, a colleague from Akuafo Hall of the University of Ghana, told me on the telephone that he would see to all the administrative and logistic procedures and that I could wait till daylight broke before going over to the hospital.

The rest, as the saying goes, is history. The day of the funeral was a never-to-be-forgotten experience. The demonstration of love and sympathy from people far and near was overwhelming.

Yes, they that sow in tears shall reap in joy.

She went home to be with the Lord she put her trust in after leaving her imprints in the sands of time.

THE AUTHOR

Kofi Otutu Adu Labi, a lawyer, was educated at Ofori Panin, Achimota School, University of Ghana and the University of Bradford School of Management. He has also studied at Georgetown University Law Center, the International Law Institute (Washington DC), the Cranfield School of Management and London Business School. He served as Advisor under two Governors of the Bank of Ghana.

He started his banking career at the then SSB Bank (now Societé Generale Ghana) as a pioneering staff in 1976 and was the founding head of the Legal Department, before rising to the position of General Manager. He has extensive experience in project management, negotiations, human capital management and corporate strategy.

He has held a number of directorships including Commissioner, Securities and Exchange Commission Ghana; the National Pensions Regulatory Authority, Taysec Construction, Taysec Properties, Scripture Union Ghana, Victory Presbyterian Church School and the Bible Society of Ghana. His current directorships include Trustee, Presbyterian Church of Ghana Education Foundation; Zoomlion Domestic Services and The BEIGE Bank (BEIGE Capital).

The author has served as a resource person at a number of events, including the 1st World Bank Conference on Financial Infrastructure (Rio de Janeiro 2011) and the 4th United Nations Conference on Less Developed Countries (Istanbul 2011).

The author is a raconteur and also a teacher and elder of the Presbyterian Church of Ghana. He has served as Elder and Senior Presbyter at Dansoman Emmanuel Congregation and Victory Congregation, Fafraha.

He has been married to Elioenai since 1978 and they have five adult children and two grandchildren.

www.ingramcontent.com/pod-product-compliance
Lightning Source LLC
LaVergne TN
LVHW021342080426
835508LV00020B/2076